The Good
Samaritan

Sonny Harris

WestBow
P R E S S
A DIVISION OF THOMAS NELSON

WestBow Press books may be ordered through booksellers or by contacting:

WestBow Press
A Division of Thomas Nelson
1663 Liberty Drive
Bloomington, IN 47403
www.westbowpress.com
1-(866) 928-1240

Because of the dynamic nature of the Internet, any web addresses or links contained in this book may have changed since publication and may no longer be valid. The views expressed in this work are solely those of the author and do not necessarily reflect the views of the publisher, and the publisher hereby disclaims any responsibility for them.

Any people depicted in stock imagery provided by Thinkstock are models, and such images are being used for illustrative purposes only.

Certain stock imagery © Thinkstock.

ISBN: 978-1-4497-2304-0 (sc)
ISBN: 978-1-4497-2306-4 (hc)
ISBN: 978-1-4497-2303-3 (e)

Library of Congress Control Number: 2011913429

Printed in the United States of America

WestBow Press rev. date: 08/09/2011

Introduction

The man lay face down in his own vomit. The dark, damp room was filled with such a vile odor that those who didn't need to be in the room did not enter. I had to be there to assist the coroner in taking pictures, securing any identification, and trying to find any evidence of a family member that we could contact. I had done this a hundred times, a hundred different places, with a hundred different faces, and they all shared the same common fate. They had died alone. There was no family standing by the bedside. There were no people sitting in a waiting room outside an intensive care unit. They died lacking any human tenderness, compassion, or reason. It seemed to me that surely there must have been someone who knew of these people's troubles; that knew them in a better time in their life when they were on their feet and doing well. There must have been someone who once loved them or even cared enough to remember their name.

Our society is at peace with leaving humanity to its own sins. We offer these anonymous people a parting gesture of good will. We give them a name, Mr. John Doe or Ms. Jane Doe. It makes us feel good about ourselves and what we believe, and we like feeling good about what we believe. I used to be pretty sure about what I believed.

I am not so sure anymore. Some things are definite. Some things are so hidden from my understanding I don't know what to believe.

I would see things as a paramedic, deputy coroner, nurse, and as a pastor that would shake the very foundations of my deepest beliefs. It would be this wonderful journey of life that would carry me past the dead, past the grand old South's refusal to die, and past the safety of religion's boundaries. With both eyes wide open, I raced through these precious days running alongside the path God had chosen for me and finding myself lost and wandering in my own pious direction. I reached the place of certain destruction and yet found grace's path of restoration and comfort.

What we believe must be based upon the truth. Truth must be tasted, smelled, and touched to find its way into our beliefs. Our beliefs do not happen overnight and can change with time, but the truth never changes. We may choose to ignore the truth to make what has happened acceptable or to understand why something has happened, but the truth can never be changed. Our beliefs are based on what we believe to be true. In a court of law, we swear to tell the truth, the whole truth, and nothing but the truth, so help us God.

. This expresses man's effort to tell the truth, knowing that one day God Himself will reveal the truth in every soul's life. Who, what, when, where, and how will be divinely revealed and judged in measure and merit. Moving back through time and distance realities become distorted by personal vestment, belief, and ability. Truth becomes relative to experiences and belief.

This is a story woven in the tapestry of truth and imagination revealing the truest proof of life, imperfection. Like a coat of many colors the random pieces of life lay like weathered fabrics revealing what the world has cast against it. The imperfections are recognized by the imperfect, ignored by the poor, and treasured by the soul who finds beauty and warmth in the life God has given.

Rifling through the pockets of the dead, items never intended to be seen are examined for any information that might tell us who this person was. Plastic bags filled with smelly, wrinkled clothes are stacked by the bed. Empty beer cans and whiskey bottles are piled in the center of a small table. Expired medication bottles reveal a name that may or may not belong to the deceased. Neighbors are questioned, landlords sought, and 9-1-1 records pulled for this address are reviewed for police or EMS response. Recovering the dead person's true identity and cause of death may take several days. Until then, he or she bears the name of the unknown dead, Mr. or Ms. John Doe.

This name is written on the identification tag and tied to the big toe. The body is wrapped in a clean white cotton sheet and placed in a plastic body bag where another identification tag is attached. The body is transported to the county morgue and placed in an stainless steel refrigerated chest. The sliding tray bearing the deceased's remains also bears our parting gesture of good will toward Mr. or Ms. John Doe. The tray is pushed inward, the door closed, and the slamming sound of the latches ushers in the silence of death. It is true that dead men tell no tales. So if a story of one's journey in this world is to be told it must be told in life, so help us God.

Chapter I

"In the Beginning, God Created"

I had worked all night on the graveyard shift at a local hospital where I worked as a "hospital technician," the modern name for an orderly. I was seventeen years old, six foot three, and around one hundred twenty pounds, ten of which, I am sure, was my hair. I had three brothers and a sister who lived with my mother and stepfather in a small mobile home. For about two years I had been living with my cousin, whose parents had died. During those years when I should have been getting ready for college or a trade, I was doing everything but that. It was the time of my life I refer to as "the movement." Everything and everybody was moving so fast, in so many directions, you just chose one and went. For my cousin and me, it was Budweiser, drag racing, and girls. My cousins were older, and many times I ended up doing things that were entirely beyond my developmental stage of life. At the age of sixteen, I was doing whatever I wanted, and all I wanted to do was party.

During the week, we worked at our jobs and brought home modest paychecks. On the weekend, we would spend every penny of it on alcohol, grass, and girls. The party did not last forever, like I thought it would. Of the five of us who spent those two years of our lives together, only two would live past their twenty-first birthday. One would be killed in a motorcycle accident when his head struck a concrete drainage pipe. Another one would die in a head-on collision in Alabama, and still another would be killed in an ambush during his second week in Vietnam. I still ask myself why God allowed me to live, but alive I was. I was still as careless, still as stupid, still as free to do whatever I wanted to do, but that morning as I ate, I would see something that would change the course of my life forever.

The steam rising from the bowl of grits that sat beside my eggs and bacon required some serious pursed-lip blowing to cool them. It was through this Southern mist that I would catch my first glimpse of the love of my life. It was a long, bright red-and-white ambulance, a new Cadillac that shined like a diamond in a showcase window. The large chrome siren that was mounted on the fender reflected the sun, demanding my attention. It stood like a majestic carriage ready for a parade. It was the most beautiful thing that I had ever seen in my life.

With her beauty, she brought a thousand questions. I had seen ambulances all my life but knew very little about them. I knew the men who drove them were called ambulance drivers. I knew that they raced down the country roads and city streets of my town. I knew that their sirens warned of a danger that everyone seemed to understand without question: if you did not get out of their way, they could kill you. They flew. The survival of the ambulance company depended on whose ambulance arrived at the scene first, how many people they could stuff in it, and how fast they could be ready for the next call. I did not know all this as I sat and finished my breakfast, but I would learn. I would learn everything.

It was the early seventies, and the requirements for operating an ambulance service then were far from what EMS providers maintain today. As I walked across the street toward the two-story brick building where the ambulance was parked, I made a list of questions that I should ask.

I began to climb a circular staircase and knew that all the answers to my questions would be at the top . Someone was snoring really loudly with periods of apnea that I was sure was this person's last breath. An old-fashioned office door was open at the top of the stairs. Two small rooms served as office, sleeping quarters, and storage garage for this two-vehicle company. Behind the desk sat a huge man, his unshaven chin resting on his chili-stained white uniform shirt. I stood and looked at him for what seemed like an eternity before I could find the courage to wake him. I took a deep breath and knocked very gently on the glass door. I'd never seen someone wake up so fast in my life! Instantly he was awake and, in his professional voice, introducing himself as he extended this huge right hand. This was Big Jim.

Big Jim was six feet five inches tall. He weighed somewhere close to 290 pounds. He was the biggest man I had ever seen. He spoke with a gentle tone of voice. His slow, Southern words seemed to float without any colloquial effort whatsoever. I was really nervous, and he asked several questions, but his manner was accepting and gracious for any answer that I provided. He was like many Southern funeral home directors that I would meet over the years. I didn't know it then, but I would learn that his father had run a funeral home in southern Alabama until his death. Big Jim had grown up hearing his father's voice soothing the grief-stricken. It was Big Jim's largest trait: the ability to remain calm and reassuring even in the most tense moments of uncertainty.

Big Jim asked some very general questions and then called the owner of the ambulance service on the radio. He asked him to return to the office to complete the interview. The owner was a young man, around thirty years old. This was his business, but his full-time job was working as a disc jockey at a popular radio station in town. He was a short man with a receding hairline. He wore gold-rimmed sunglasses and carried a cigar between his teeth, only removing it to speak. He walked with a cocky strut. You knew you were going to be impressed by this man because he was already so impressed with himself, it was obvious. He carried a large key ring on his belt and a long silver chain attached to his wallet. Over his shirt and tie he wore a waist-length white cotton jacket. The American First Aid patch had been sewn above his left breast pocket. He was everything that Big Jim was not. His voice was deep, and as he would articulate, he would point and wave the cigar in grand gestures. I never heard him speak in a regular voice. It was as if he was on the radio twenty-four hours a day, and he had an opinion about everything. He drove a green Pontiac Grand Prix and had a two-way radio installed in it so he could monitor the ambulance business. He also carried a .38-caliber pistol in the center console of whatever vehicle he was in. He was a character in every sense of the word. He arrived and completed the interview. The entire event lasted less than thirty minutes. I was hired and scheduled for my first class in the ambulance business.

Today so many different special certifications are required, coupled with at least an associate's degree as a paramedic. Back then, it was a first-aid card, a driver's license, and no outstanding warrants. I could not believe it! I was going to be an ambulance driver. The class was the next morning, and it lasted three hours. I learned how to make a splint out of a magazine, to wrap a roller bandage, and to change an oxygen bottle. That was it. My medical training to begin this career that would span the course of my life lasted only three hours. Coffee and cigarette breaks probably shortened the class time to about an hour, but since I was the only student and Big Jim the only instructor, the class went rather smoothly, the way Big Jim liked things to go. His favorite expression when decisions had to be made and you would ask why was, "Don't worry about the mule, just load the wagon."

The first day on the job was so thrilling I would have worked for free. Riding through the neighborhood where I lived, I would sit up straight in the seat so anyone that might know me could see me. I was gone. I would sit by the desk and wait for the phone to ring, but I was not allowed to answer the phone. Only Big Jim answered the phone; only Big Jim would drive the ambulance. Every time the phone rang, my heart raced. I could hardly breathe. If it were a request from the city police dispatcher, we would race down the stairs to the ambulance. It was impressive. People would pull over to the right side of the road and stop, allowing us to pass them. It made what I did seem important. People would stare as we passed, and it was important that our facial expressions be of grave concern and urgency. Big Jim taught me that early on. He would always say, "People will not care if you mess up, just as long as you're nice about it." Big Jim knew more about people than he ever did about emergency medicine, but some things he taught me about being an ambulance driver were priceless. We carried a black doctor's bag in the ambulance containing bandages, scissors, a blood pressure cuff, and a stethoscope. We also carried stethoscopes around our necks. I didn't know how to use them; didn't know how to take a blood pressure. But they looked good, so we carried them. When the pressure was on and it seemed liked the thing to do, we would place the stethoscope on the person's chest and say, "Um, we need to get this man to the hospital." It gave the general appearance of knowledge and concern, and besides, that's why they called an ambulance. So everybody was happy, except the nurses. The nurses knew. They knew everything.

While there would be some nurses that had insight as to where emergency medicine was headed in the future and provided invaluable training, most considered us a stepchild of medicine and questioned our every advancement in training. You have to remember that this was during the time when nurses still wore white uniforms and hats. Black stripes on the uniforms for the registered nurses and blue for the practical nurses. Their uniforms were starched white cotton skirts and blouses. They were not the Trauma Mamas and Papas you see across America today. They were from the old school where an ambulance driver was just that, an ambulance driver—nothing more and nothing less. In the early seventies, they were right, ambulance drivers had a lot to learn. However, over the course of the next thirty years the paramedic would have more experience and training than many emergency room nurses and even some physicians. But it didn't happen overnight.

Changes came quickly and regularly in the field of emergency medical services. Equipment was developed so fast that it seemed like a new item was placed on the ambulance every day. The Cadillacs vanished and were replaced with the modular ambulance. A fiberglass box that had doors on it was mounted on the bed of a truck. The trucks were more practical because they could carry more equipment, but they always seemed to lack the class that the big red-and-white ambulance that I fell in love with had. Change also affected the ambulance driver. He was becoming extinct. Many would find the educational requirements too hard, the hours too long, or the work too demanding. Big Jim would quit early in his career and start selling life insurance. He would die in the back of one of those modular ambulances in full cardiac arrest ten years after I had met him. The owner of the first ambulance service I had worked for was shot in the head by a jealous husband who found him with his wife at a beach house. I can still remember his introduction for his daily radio program, "Taking you downtown with the Motown sound cause if loving you is wrong baby, I don't wanna be right!"

Faces too numerous to remember vanished in the early days of emergency medical services. The ambulance drivers vanished and were replaced by the ninety-day wonders who were the new graduates from the technical school paramedic programs. They walked down the halls of emergency rooms with every tool known to man hanging from their belts. They sauntered in and out of places lost in their arrogance as they wore uniforms of every description. Their pants had eight pockets, each filled with a new tool or an extra pair of sunglasses that hid their inexperience. Their boots were NASA- approved and their hats seemed to fit even the biggest head. Their war stories were always longer, the crashes bigger, the fires hotter, and their length of service shorter. The common element that the ninety-day wonder and the ambulance driver shared was reason. You either had a reason to be doing this kind of work or you didn't. If there was not a natural ability to remain calm when those around you panicked, not compassion in your efforts, not a thirst for knowledge that would enable you to better take care of people, not a physical ability to withstand stress and make life and death decisions in a second, then you just quit. From the footprints of the ambulance driver would step the modern paramedic and rescue specialist. I was an ambulance driver and the road to the future lay ahead. There would be no training that would prepare me for what some days held, no warning of their perilous and heartbreaking moments. I was an ambulance driver, but I became something else along the way. What that was is for others to judge.

Chapter II

"From the Rib"

Life seemed good as an ambulance driver. I worked at the hospital and at the ambulance service. My life had become busier than I liked, but it helped take my mind off how much I missed home. The home I missed was where I grew up with my three brothers and sister. I had left home when I was sixteen to live with my cousin. The trailer where my family lived was small and the current stepfather number one was not my favorite. My mother was a wonderful mother whose heart was so full of forgiveness she could love you no matter how badly you had disappointed her. I guess that's why she stayed with my father for fifteen years of torment. He was seventeen years old when he was wounded in Korea and returned to the states with half a stomach. He would keep the remaining half full of alcohol the better part of his life. I can still hear my mother's voice pleading with him to come in the house and be quiet before the police came, but the police always came. They always took him away, sometimes for the night, maybe a week, maybe a month. He would sit in jail and have three meals a day while his wife and five children ate biscuits and gravy for breakfast and supper. There were family members that came by and offered assistance. Some had lost patience long ago with Mother for staying with him. But what else could she do? She was the mother of five children.

There was never a question in her heart what a mother should do. Her mother had died when she was four years old. She grew up on a west Georgia farm surrounded by family that loved and cared for her but was devoid of a mother's care. I have an old picture of her when she was four years old. She was standing outside an old wooden house and there were two other little girls by her side. She was holding onto the two children. You can see the sadness in her eyes even then. The tight grip with which she held onto those children would be the same at the birth of each of her children. She just grabbed each one of us as we came and never let go. It did not matter how old you were, what you had accomplished, or how you had failed, she loved her children without question or measure.

Stepfathers who thought they had achieved a status that allowed them to decide which one of her children would or would not receive help if they needed it were soon added to the list of the departed. It certainly was not fair to these men . They were, for the most part, good and honest men. They were blue collar and white collar workers. Each came with their past life experiences and hopes for the future, and each adored my mother. However, they failed to understand that these five children and the grandchildren who would follow were her sole responsibility. Even as her children would grow older and see her sacrifices robbing herself of a better life, she would simply ignore husbands and do whatever she could to help the one that was in a tight spot. I recalled these memories from time to time and the experiences of my childhood . Our life was not like the Walton's tales of trials and moral justice. It was at times heartbreaking, hopeless, and without direction. However, it would be the past which would guide me through many more difficult and trying days ahead.

I was a lonely ambulance driver. Some of my cousins had died and others had moved on in life. College, marriage, jobs, all seemed to dismantle our circle of nomads that had waged our own private time of civil unrest during "the movement." None of us had gone to jail, except me. I spent thirty days in a county jail for calling in a false alarm at a place where my cousin and I worked. Someone had called in a bomb threat the day before at work and the company sent us home early. My cousin was working and there were these girls. There were always these girls. I thought if I called they would send him home and we could party. I was no terrorist and confessed my sins to a friendly policeman when he came to the house the next day. He knew which house to come to because I had asked the operator to break the line because it was busy when I called. The stupidity of a seventeen-year-old coupled with the effects of golden grain alcohol and pot made me easy pickings for the police. In a day when rotary phones were used this was a coup for modern day police work and Ma Bell. The friendly policeman became very official and acted as he had just solved the biggest case since the JFK investigation. Everybody made such a big deal out of it that even to this day I have to explain it when filling out certain applications. It was a big deal to my family as many of them worked at this company. Some of them were supervisors, and it was a great source of embarrassment. Several family members were at court with me. They wept as I was lead away by the sheriff's deputy. I always had an ability to do the stupidest things in the largest way.

Upon my arrival at the county jail, I saw arms hanging out of the barred windows. Some men were hollering out of the windows as I got out of the car at the receiving bay. I tried not to listen and ignored the pleasant invitations to share their bunks with them, but I was shaking like a leaf when I walked up to the desk of the head jailer. He took the papers and slowly read the charge and sentence document. He read my name out loud twice. He put his glasses on his huge nose and asked, "You got a name like a fellow I used to know. You named after your daddy, boy?" "Yes," I replied. "Thought I recognized the name," he uttered. I did not know it then, but God was already looking after me. This man had locked up my father many times for many reasons. He knew all there was to know about my family's history. He knew that Daddy was an alcoholic, and how he used to throw all our furniture in the yard because one of Mother's sisters or brothers had given it to us. He also knew that my father was arrested so many times for driving under the influence that if the police saw him getting in a car drunk, they'd just go ahead and lock him up before he started driving. He saw the bruises on Mother's arms and the tears on her face. He even knew about the last night we lived with my father.

I was almost thirteen years old that night and had seen my father do many wicked things to his family. I had watched him push my mother and my brothers and sister to the floor. Mostly I had watched him push me. That last night he was demanding an audience for his drunken psychotic ramblings. He would curse and say horrible things about my mother's family and about us, like how we were the children of a whore and that he wasn't our father. His vile anger came with more regularity then as did his physical abuse. My younger brother was twelve. We were just children, but we thought we were old enough and big enough to stand up to him. We knew when he was drunk he could barely stand up, let alone defend himself. My mother had already told us not to do anything stupid and get ourselves or others hurt. She must have lived in constant fear every Friday because Daddy got paid on Fridays, and when he got home he would be drunk and mad about something. Mad that he had to give all his money to pay the rent or the light bill, and that all Mother did was sit at home, and tell her brothers and sisters how bad he was. Nothing could have been further from the truth. Why she defended him and chose to stay with him was beyond my ability to understand. I knew things were getting worse, and I had the knots on my head to prove it.

One night I was awakened by his staggering effort to come into the bedroom I shared with my three brothers and sister. I watched him raise the covers from my sister's bed and lift her night clothes to look at her. The next morning I told my sister about what had happened, and I assumed that she told Mother. From that day forward when he came home drunk, I tried to stay out of his sight. Sometimes I would sit under the house until I heard his ravings grow quiet or my sister softly calling us boys to bed. She was the oldest and the boss, and we followed her without question. That night would be no different.

It was a Saturday evening and Daddy had not been home for over a week. He had been painting a house with another man, and they had completed the work and gotten paid for it. It must have been a big house because I remember my mother was so proud that his share was going to be three hundred dollars. But when Friday came and went and then another, he still had not come home. When he would do things like this, and he did them often, my mother would always find a way to provide a meal. She had learned one thing about him. She could not always depend on him to take care of her children so she had to.

Mother would take in ironing. My older cousin and his wife, who lived with my grandfather, would bring by baskets of clothes for her to iron. He and his wife worked at the cotton mill in town, and they drove a new Plymouth convertible. They would pull up in front of the house, and my cousin would sound the horn. My mother would go out and take the clothes, and they would speed away in that bright red shiny car. She would iron for two or three days until she completed her task. They brought shirts, pants, pillowcases, blouses, crocheted tablecloths, curtains, and even undershirts. If it was machine washable, they brought it, and she ironed it. My sister and I would help her from time to time when she was busy cooking or something. I've never asked anybody to iron anything for me in my life. I can take care of my own but I could not take care of what that night would bring.

Mother had been paid for her ironing and as was our custom, my brother and I were sent to the store for RC colas and Moon Pies. It was the only treat in the world as far as we were concerned. We carried the carton of bottled drinks at a brisk pace so they would still be cold when we got home. One would carry the drinks, the other the paper sack containing six chocolate Moon Pies. We would sit on the front porch around Mother, and she would smile as we all ate the treats and drank the colas. Mother would sit with us until we had finished, and as she waited she would tell us about the days of her childhood. She told us how she and her sister would visit an aunt that lived near their home. That this aunt would sit and eat an apple or some treat during their visit and never offer them a crumb. That must have deeply hurt my mother's feelings because when she told it, she would always do so in a slow, quiet voice. At the conclusion of the story, she would always say the same thing, "You know, that wasn't right." She had shared that story again with us this evening, and we had listened as if it were the first time we had heard it. Mother loved to share her stories. She loved her older brothers and sisters, and in her childhood they were her mother in many ways.

We were sitting on the front porch steps laughing and enjoying this wonderful time, when we heard a familiar sound that silenced our laughter. It was Daddy singing, "I went down to the river to watch the fish swim by, but when I got to the river the dog gone river was dry." Then we heard him hollering at the widow woman who lived two houses below us. He was screaming at her, "Poot on you, poot on you and the police too!" Our silence told each of us that this was going to be a long night.

Mother sent us inside to get ready for bed. It was not even near bed time, but we knew this was the best. She tried to shield us from his insanity as best she could, but there was no hiding place in our house, not even in our neighborhood. Even as children we could recognize a night the police were going to be coming to our house. My father's loud ranting would set the tempo for the evening. The louder he became, the sooner the neighbors would call the police if they had a phone. Most of our neighbors did not because they were poor and had their own problems. The last thing they needed was Daddy standing in front of their house screaming. It must have been a tight month in the neighborhood because no one called the police that night.

He entered the house carrying a sack of cheap peach wine. That meant that he had spent the money he had earned painting and was coming home broke. I can't remember everything that he said to my mother, but he was crazy that night. He was driven by an indwelling desire to destroy our family and everything that was in our modest home. The television was the first to go. He threw it onto the floor, and it scared Mother to death. She had always thought that it would blow up if dropped. He broke every chair at the kitchen table and then turned his attention to us. He seemed to know that this was the one thing that would summon a fight from my mother. As he stood throwing plates against the kitchen wall and cursing my mother and her family, he saw me, shook his fist at me, and told me to come to him. My mother leapt between him and the doorway to our bedroom. She stood there and told him that he if wanted to hurt her babies that he would have to kill her first. He seemed to welcome the idea. He shoved her to the floor and ran into our bedroom. The five of us ran out the other door with my sister carrying my youngest brother.

We circled around in the house, running from room to room with him chasing and shouting. I passed the stove and noticed water heating in a pot on the stove. My mother used it to dissolve the starch she used on clothes she had to iron. I stopped. When my father approached, I told him to stop and leave us alone. He laughed and mocked my feeble attempt at bravery. The water on the stove was hot but not boiling. At that time I wished it had been boiling just like the fires of hell when I threw it on his head. He slipped down as he jumped back. That gave Mother the time to collect her brood and run out the front door. We did not know where we were running to, only what we were running from.

None of us had shoes on because we were supposed to be getting ready for bed. Mother had taken my youngest brother in her arms.

She kept looking around making sure everyone was there and was managing to keep up. I could see fear in her eyes that I had never seen before. I know now that it was not only the fear of my father's insanity, but also the fear of uncertainty that lay ahead of us in the darkness. The only light to guide us came from the moon, and by it I could see the tears as they ran down her face. Her hair was in disarray, and she kept pulling her torn dress up onto her shoulders. We ran and ran and ran. The pounding of our bare feet on the highway was silenced only by the beating of our hearts. No deer ever bounded for safety as we did that night. No solider in battle knew of a greater effort to seek shelter from harm's way than we did. No messenger ever bore a sadder message than had been laid at the door of our home that horrible night. It was gone, all gone. Our childhood and home as we knew it was gone forever.

My father cursed and threw rocks at us as we ran. He threatened to kill us if we didn't come back home. But we could not go back because our home was gone. Everything home stood for disappeared in the darkness. There would never be another place that we as children would recognize as home. In the early days of our flight to safety and freedom, we would become nomads as we traveled from one gracious gesture of a relative to another. In time, that night's horror would lessen in our memories. The details blurred by the sights of the freedom that we found in our youth. The loss of innocence , however, could never be hidden in our hearts. The effort to fill this emptiness would take each of us into his or her own life. Some efforts would be valiant yet tragic, others simply a mirror of what was. Some of my siblings chose to ignore the magnitude of that event, but none could forgot those moments of childhood poverty. Poverty that once caused five children to remember the vast riches in a place called home. We remembered it all, but some remembered only the source of our family's demise, my father.

The chief jailer informed me that I would work as a trustee during my thirty day sentence. I would not be placed on a felony cell tier, but instead joined the group of men known as trustees that worked in the jail. The jobs were hard, but it was the price you paid to remain safe. We would get out of bed at four thirty every morning, take a shower, and get ready to prepare breakfast. My first day at work I pushed the heavy metal cart to each cell block. Through the tiny square window I could see the men as they peered out, each trying to see the faces of the men who brought the meals. They reminded me of the hunting hound dogs that my uncle owned. Each growling and pushing their way forward to get their tray and their only glance outside of that cell block.

There were about forty men in each cell block. The bunk beds were old army- style metal frames with plastic mattresses. The men were given one sheet, one blanket, and one pillow. If they lost these items, they were not replaced and it probably meant that they had lost more than linen. I looked at the men in the back of this pressing line. They looked scared and small. When they took their tray, they acted as if they wanted to say something and constantly kept looking over their shoulders. None of these young men ever spoke a word.

When I used to feed my uncle's hounds, I would have to remain in the pen and make sure every dog had the chance to eat. If one did not, the larger and meaner hounds would fight the smaller hounds and take their food. The smaller hounds put up a snarling effort, but without my assistance it would mean a violent fight and no food. The situation in jail was not much different. It was a hidden world from the streets of our small town; a real jail where men who had been charged with state or federal indictments awaited court dates. Many were hardened criminals who had already been in prison. There were no separate cells so the bad and the not so bad were together. They were cast into these cells as room became available. This would be my only view of these cells as I was not asked to push the meal cart again. I believe the sergeant wanted me to see what I had been spared from. I shall never forget his act of compassion.

The meals were served in stainless steel trays. Each tray had three sections: a section for the eggs, a section for the grits, and a section for the biscuit and piece of fried pork called fat back. The head trustee was a black man who had been charged and convicted of murder. He had served most of his sentence and had been paroled. During his parole he had been arrested for robbery. He had been in jail a year waiting for his day in court. He was not a man to mess with.

One afternoon he had found dried grits in some of the trays that I had washed. He cursed at me and told me to wash all the trays again. I started to balk at his orders, but the look in his eyes silenced me. I washed every tray again. I had heard the other trustees say that his hearing was the next week. The closer his hearing came, the quieter and more secluded he became. Some of the trustees said he had told them he would never go back to the federal prison again. The day of the hearing came, and he showered and put on a nice dark blue suit. Later that day I watched the sheriff's department car pull into the receiving bay at the jail. He was handcuffed and shackled at the ankles. He shuffled along as they lead him back inside the jail. Then they brought him to the trustee area where he followed as the deputies gathered his belongings. He had been found guilty of the robbery and the violation of his parole. He had received twenty years for the robbery and also had to complete the remaining twenty years of his original sentence. Forty years total. They had practically sentenced him to life without parole. There was no expression on his face. He was considered too great a risk for escape and had to be placed in the general population until his transfer the following week. I shall always remember the hopelessness I saw in his eyes. I shall never forget the hopelessness in the eyes of the many men I had seen through those tiny windows as I had passed out trays.

Thirty days came and went and I was leaving. My debt to society had partially been paid. The eleven months of probation was all that remained. Mother had came every Saturday during the morning visitation period. She had not missed a one. She brought ten dollars every visit and passed it through the fence to me. I could see the concern she had on her face, but I could also see her deepest love for me in her teary eyes as she departed each week. She would always say, "I'll see you next week, son. It's almost over." I don't know what causes a boy to fail to understand how much his mother loves him. How he can pass by the dearest moments of his life and find other things so much more important. But he can. I did. The morning I got out of jail, Mother had cake and ice cream waiting for me at home. Instead I chose to have a girl pick me up and spent that afternoon with her. When I arrived home, she hugged my neck, kissed my cheek, and told me she loved me, never asking where I had been or what I had been doing. I wished I had seen the cake before it was cut. I wished I had gone home that morning. What a jerk I had been. I wished I could go back home and do things differently.

I stood and looked over the ambulance to make sure that I had not missed a spot. I washed both ambulances every shift I worked. It would be in these solitary moments that I missed my family. I wished I could go back in time and everything would be different. My father would not be an alcoholic and my family would not have to endure the uncertainty of the future.

I lied to myself a lot at that time. I lied all the way through school. I denied what my father had done in the neighborhood that last weekend at home. I lied about why the police were at my house. I insisted that I just was not hungry at lunch at school. There were no food stamp programs during my childhood. The state did provide a free lunch program for children when I was in the fourth grade. I had to present my bright green card to the lunchroom cashier. She lived down the street from where I had lived with my parents. She would always frown when I presented the card and hold it up to the light like I had forged it or something. She made sure every other student in line saw it. I used it the first week, but I just could not bare the daily humiliation, so I lied about being hungry. I lied about my shoes, my hand-me-down clothes, the reason I could not join any teams that required buying uniforms or special shoes. I lied about everything to everybody. It became as natural as breathing. When I moved in with my cousin who had lost both parents, it didn't stop. Then I had to lie about my age, my education, what my future was, and even worse, I lied to myself by believing that this was the way to acceptance. My cousins used to say that if I came in the house wet and said it was raining, they would have to go outside and look because I may have wet myself with the hose. I was a good liar, and people believed me. The worst thing was sometimes I believed my lies.

The fact that I was lonely was not a lie. Stepfather number one and my family filled the trailer we lived in to its limit. I had rented an apartment in town close to the hospital. It was a dump with one bedroom and one bath in the basement of a house. I was not used to such privacy. It was making me crazy. I had a telephone but no one called. Everyone who meant something to me had moved away to college or gotten married. I met a lot of people working at the hospital and on the ambulance. Meeting a lot of people meant I had to tell a lot of lies. I don't know why I thought I could not be honest about myself—who I was and what my hopes and dreams were—but I could not. Instead, when I met older girls or other guys I would automatically lie. I don't remember exactly how many lies I told during this period. There were so many to so many people. But the right lie to the right person at the right time in your life can alter the course of the rest of your life.

I don't remember where I met this girl, but it was probably at the hospital or somewhere on the ambulance. I told her I was studying medicine and was going to be a doctor. I guess we dated. I can't really remember, nor do I remember asking her to marry me. I was drinking and smoking pot so much, I remember very little of it. It's hard to really believe that someone somewhere along the line could not have seen the insanity of my youth.

My family bought wedding presents, tuxes were rented, and the wedding was set. I guess my family loved me and hoped that this would be something good for me. The day of the wedding came faster than the lie that had come out of my mouth. But here I was on my wedding day, and the girl I was to marry believed that I was going to be doctor. My cousin, who was serving as my best man, and I stood outside the church and smoked pot. We just made it inside the church as the parents were being seated. I remember telling him it was too late now. He did not know of the great wrong I had done to this girl and her family by lying. Only I knew. When I told him it was too late he replied, "The car's outside, man, let's go." I wish I had listened to him.

The marriage was short-lived after the girl's father learned of my lie. He was a gentleman about it, and I remember his concern for his daughter. He encouraged me to remain with his daughter, and he would help us. He was soft-spoken and a fine man. I had lied, but somehow his and his wife's hope for their daughter's happiness outweighed any of my wrongdoings. I stayed only a short time. I had lied, but the truth was I didn't love his daughter. My lie had broken too many hearts and caused too much trouble. There was no defense for my actions, but there was a remedy. This remedy was not delivered by the man who had performed the ceremony. Had he come to me and presented the gospel who knows what might have been. Whether he was ever made aware of the brevity of the marriage, I cannot say. All I can say for certain is that I never saw this minister again in a pastoral role. Satan had launched his offensive attack and had wounded as many as he could, yet there came no news of a balm in Gilead. Like many youth in the seventies, I was left to my own demise.

I continued to work for both places for a while, but the ambulance service was having a hard time meeting payroll. I stayed with this ambulance service until it went out of business. The county had begun its first emergency medical technician program for the local rescue department. I found myself again standing outside a church smoking a joint prior to a wedding service. As absurd as it may sound, I don't remember asking this girl to marry me either. But I don't remember a lot of things that happened back then.

This time it was a wedding at a church in South Carolina. I had met this girl at a fourth of July party, and in September we were married. There were no lies. I had no reason to lie anymore because I had came to the place where I did not care what people thought. I was not driving an ambulance at this time, but was working as an electrician's helper. I really missed the ambulance work, and my wife missed her home and parents in South Carolina so we moved.

Chapter III

"The Garden of Eden"

The South Carolina town was a small rural town that sat about thirty miles from the coast. I remember asking myself why someone built a road right out in the middle of these woods. It was like stepping back in a time machine. The town had one of everything: one red light, one grocery store, one pharmacy, one bank. The people were characters who took great pride in their effort to retain a self-imposed colloquial speech and custom. It was referred to as the low country, and I was feeling kind of low being there. Jobs were limited, and it seemed that if you were not related to someone, your application for employment was a waste of time. I worked at a couple of places for a short time, but I was an ambulance driver and missed it. It was by happenstance that I passed by the neighboring county's EMS headquarters building.

I stopped and filled out an application and was hired that same morning. I was officially hired by a county-run emergency medical service as an ambulance driver. I did not have an emergency medical technician's license, but I could start as a driver and complete the next available course. The EMT course instructor worked for my county's service. He was a pleasant man who assured me that I would have no problem completing the course. I could not believe it. I mean these guys had real uniforms with patches on the shoulders, not just sewed on the pocket of a white jacket. The ambulances were Chevrolet vans with raised fiberglass roofs. You could stand up in these things. They were white with an orange strip around the complete vehicle. The ambulances and programs this service had would be typical of many ambulance services throughout the country. It was the very beginning of our country's emergency medical service as we know it today. It was the real beginning of my profession. The low country was looking up.

I found so many things in Georgetown County that I liked. There was a river close by that was the most beautiful river I had ever seen. The black tide water bathed the huge cypress trees and lily pads on its shoreline. The river produced fish with names I had never heard of before like mud-fish, rock bass, and maw-mouths. It was a fisherman's paradise. The entire surrounding area was a rural haven for all types of hunters.

There were deer hunters who enjoyed a hunting season that went from September 1 until January 1. They had trucks with dog boxes in the rear bed of the truck. Each truck had long CB-radio antennas attached to it. It seemed that each man took great pride in the length of his antenna and his ability to be able to communicate. There were four wheel drives, two wheel drives, and some trucks that needed to be pushed before the hunting day was over. It was a sport that was a tradition, not just a mere sport.

Men would join a hunting club that leased a lot of wooded property from paper companies or local farmers. They would build some type of clubhouse where everyone would gather on hunting mornings and plan their day. Each man brought his truck filled with his hounds. That was what the hunting was really about. It was not the trucks that raced down muddy roads or the chattering on the CB radios. It was the chase. It was who's hound struck the track and which hound was leading the pack when it crossed the road. I had learned a lot about hounds from my mother's youngest brother. He had several fox hounds that he raised and hunted with on Friday nights. It was not the traditional fox chase that one sees in England.

This hunting was done at night. You simply took the dogs to the woods and turned them loose and listened to the chase. It was easy to tell what they were chasing. If it was a deer, the dogs would go out of hearing distance and never come back. That meant you had to leave the comfort of the fire and attempt to get in front of the pack in order to catch them. My uncle and another hunter would disagree about whose dog had jumped the fox and which dog was barking on the track. It was a serious thing that could only be settled by walking down dirt roads with flashlights in hand. As the hounds came, you would turn off your flashlight and wait. When you could hear the hounds running through the woods toward the area where you were, you would then turn on your flashlight and sight the leading hounds. The confirmation that your hound was leading the pack, or that several of your dogs were in the chase was a source of great pride. The man who had called his dog as the hound who jumped the fox would yell "Strike! , that's Chief" would face total humiliation if Chief never showed up at the roadway. My uncle was seldom displeased by the performance of his dogs. He would always find a good trait in a dog, like the ability to find the track again when the fox had given the pack the slip or the dog's ability to ignore other hounds that were on a back track. My uncle was a man's man, and he did not take his fox hunting lightly. He was a wonderful uncle who had rescued me from my grandfather's home almost every weekend right after we had left my father. It was my uncle who came that night when Father had chased us to my aunt's house. I had never seen my uncle so mad. He had his flashlight and on his belt hung his pistol. There is no question in my mind that had he found my father lurking in the bushes that night, my father's body would have been found the next morning. He was a fair and honest man and taught me more about growing up than most fathers.

He had two sons that were older than me and they, as my uncle used to call it, had their noses open. By this he meant he could get a young boy to fish and hunt with him until he reached sixteen or seventeen, but when he met girls it was all over. They were gone. He taught and lived by example the way to be a man, not a perfect man but a man. A man that people knew would do a person no wrong and would not take being wronged. I could see the respect and friendship that he had with people from many different walks of life.

He was a manager of a warehouse for a company. On the weekends he sat at the entrance of the company's lake resort and would register the employees and their guest as they came for a day of fishing or swimming. There were hundreds of peach and apple trees that grew on the green hills beside the three lakes. There was a huge pool that was fed by a spring that overflowed into a spillway, filling the three lakes. It was paradise in every sense of the word, especially for a boy who was overwhelmed by the loss of his home and father. My uncle was my dearest friend, and I loved him deeply. He would have loved this low country I found myself in and the characters who lived in it.

I had worked several weeks and had started the EMT program. It was a short three month course containing only the basics of emergency transport of the sick and injured. The department of transportation had put out a little orange book with the star of life on it. It was the Old Testament for EMS and would be changed almost on a yearly basis for the next twenty years.

I was proud to be wearing a real uniform and those cool black boots. I could hardly sleep the night before my first day, I was so excited. This was so different from the days I had spent with Big Jim. This service was the county's only ambulance service and supported two other rural counties that had only volunteer services. It was a real-life big-time ambulance service. The jaws of life did not exist at that time and any extrication from a vehicle had to be done with hand tools. There was a special course in which the only tools you were trained to use were a hammer, a bigger hammer, a screwdriver, a prize bar, a hacksaw, a jack, and wrenches. This was in the day when there were still a lot of older cars on the road and some were as heavy as tanks. New tools and pieces of equipment would come out every year. Some would survive the test, while many fell along the wayside. I thought I was going to fall by the wayside before my first month was over.

. I was in class when the sheriff's department requested an ambulance for a shooting. We were the last ambulance in service and had to respond. My instructor tried to keep me calm on the way to the call. I could hardly breathe. The red lights reflected in the early evening fog, and suddenly the ambulance slowed as we pulled into the drive. There must have been a half dozen deputy sheriff's cars leaving quickly as we pulled up. I jumped from the seat of the truck and ran to the back to get the jump kit. I was met by a man who had been the sheriff of that county for more than twenty-five years. He told me, "Put your little bag up, boy. You won't be needing it in there." He was right. I have seen dead men and women that were killed in many horrible ways. But none would remain in my memory as vividly as the scene that awaited me inside that home.

The dark green carpet was only green around the edges. The place where a man and a woman's body had been was covered with blood. The man was shot in the throat at point blank range with a 20-gauge shotgun. The woman had been shot in the jaw. She had a half moon shaped wound on her left hand as if she had been holding her hands to her face, screaming as someone shot her. The scene was horrible. What I found out later would trouble me so severely, I was unsure I wanted a job where I knew things the public would never know.

The man who was shot must have weighed 250 pounds and was over six feet tall. I learned that his seven-year-old daughter had been in the room when the murders occurred. Her father had fallen on her when he was shot, and it must have knocked her unconscious because she lay under her father's body for some time before being able to get up. She then rode her bike several miles to a relative's house for help. One of the men had shot her in the head and thought she was dead, but she actually was not shot. Her long hair contained the shot. I could not imagine the horror that this child must have experienced. These two men would share the horror with others before this evening was over.

The car ran hot again, and they stopped at a 7-11 store for water. They cooled the car and quenched their bloody thirst, shooting and killing two cashiers. They took one hostage, but let her go later after shooting her in the mouth and leaving her for dead. She suffered horrible facial trauma and would require many surgeries, but she was alive. The car ran hot again, and this time they stopped at the home of a man who happened to be a coin collector. They used the 20-gauge shotgun again and then drove to a hotel at the beach. When the vehicle was spotted, and they were surrounded by the police, the older man would turn the shotgun on himself. Many years later the younger man would die by lethal injection. I still remember his name, and I still remember who had to transport the murdered victims' bodies to the morgue.

Each one was wrapped in a white sheet and then placed in a black body bag. They were then placed in the back of a van and driven sixty-five miles to Charleston. That was the longest homicide transport I would ever have to make. I had a partner along with me, but neither of us said much. The reality of what we had seen that day hung over us, and we were not ready to talk about it, not even to each other.

Many years and murder scenes later, it seems odd. Today there are so many television programs that reveal how murders are conducted. I can't understand why people find wrongful death so interesting. These shows use actors to play the parts of the victims and the victims' family members. It is as if they want the audience to view the actual murder, and people watch it! People must watch because every season there is a new program about emergency rooms, paramedics, pathologists, or something. I believe it says that there is something profoundly wrong with our society. It's more than the typical rubberneckers who twist their necks to look at an accident scene as they drive by. It is a real murder that happened, a real accident that caused a family great pain and suffering. It is almost like every week America tunes in to see homicide photographs, bloody sidewalks, and pictures of missing victims. They want to hear every detail. The big news networks interrupt programming to show fires, shootings at schools, burning buildings, planes crashing into buildings, and they show it again and again and again. It seems odd to me that people have attempted to make money off the horror of dying victims. We as a society encourage these programs by watching them. In the beginning, it was a necessary evil to educate communities about EMS, but somewhere along the line all the public became educated about was the evil. I would see enough evil while working at this ambulance service to season and prepare me for what lay ahead.

This type of work affects people differently. Some become profoundly religious while others become cold and calloused. It causes some to build wonderful relationships with their family and friends because they see how suddenly they could lose them. For others, they allow it to destroy valued relationships because they have seen so much betrayal. I guess I have fit into both categories at one time or another.

Chapter IV

"The Burning Bush"

I completed the EMT course, and we received information about the possibility of an advanced course being developed for the state. This would allow us to have cardiac monitors, be able to start intravenous fluids, and give a few drugs. We waited. In my heart I was always an ambulance driver. I never wanted to be responsible for anyone's life. I never wanted to be doing stuff to people. I just wanted to get them to the emergency room as quickly as I could and get paid for doing it. But somehow I got sucked into this thing, and I became a ninety-day wonder.

The work became just work—the accident, the illness, the transport. All of it became just another day at work, and time passed quickly. I was a father then, and work was more important to me than it ever had been. I wanted my sons to grow up and realize that their father worked and brought home a check every payday. Their father did not disappear in the night and would always be there for them. I wanted my sons to share a hundred fishing trips with me, to listen to the hounds, and hunt white-tailed deer together. I wanted to teach them how to play a guitar and learn how to laugh, to be honest about themselves, and feel no shame. I didn't lie about the past anymore. It didn't seem necessary, but I was ashamed about a lot of things in my life. I suppose subconsciously I wanted to do something about that.

It was November and the local Free Will Baptist Church was having its fall revival. The surrounding community had been going every night including my former wife's family. I had been asked by everyone to attend, but somehow I did not consider myself a church person. I mean the only time I had spent at church in my young adult life was smoking pot outside one prior to marrying someone. No. "No, I can't go tonight," I told them. I repeated this all week during their efforts to get me to attend church. Well, Sunday morning I made a decision. I made the decision to go to church to get them off my back. That was all. I had not attended church regularly since I was a child, and some of those memories really stirred up mixed emotions.

Mother had been baptized when I was in the second grade. It's strange I know, but I remember the night she went down to the altar crying. I wondered what in the world was wrong because I could not understand it. I don't remember church anymore until much later when she took us to a house where the wall between two bedrooms had been taken down, and the people had church there. I say people, but there were only women present. The piano player was a woman, the song leader was a woman, the preacher was a woman. There were only women members. The pastor's husband attended sometimes when Daddy would attend. They painted houses together, and when they were not in jail for disorderly conduct, they would attend church. It was spiritual highs and jailhouse lows.

The pastor was a Holiness preacher and spoke in tongues. Sometimes these women would get to shouting, speaking in tongues, and running around the chairs they had set up in rows. My brothers and I would get in trouble every time because we would giggle and even fake a shout knowing that no one could hear us. However, I remember how proud I was of my father when he went to church.

He would always wear his white long-sleeved shirt and roll the sleeves up to his elbows. I thought it was a manly thing to do, but the truth was it was the only white shirt he had, and it was too small.

Nevertheless, I admired him as I sat next to him in church. It was wonderful to share this time with him. He was sober, and when he was sober, there was not a finer man. That was the reality. He was an alcoholic, and I believe it was impossible for him to remain sober for any great period of time. I've heard a lot of men say that the Lord took away their desire to drink alcohol, and they just didn't want it anymore. I'm not the Lord, and I sure don't know, but maybe these men were not alcoholics but just liked drinking liquor. You would have to had sat beside my father and look into his eyes during these church services. He looked down at the floor, and even as a child I knew he was wrestling with something bigger than he was. It made me sad. I was driving to church that Sunday morning of the revival, and these memories ran across my mind like an old favorite song you had to think about to remember the words.

The service was over, and the invitation was given. I felt no need nor any desire to go down to an altar for any reason. I shook the preacher's hand and hurried home to eat and sleep. I had worked the night before and I was very tired and sleepy. I lay in the bed with a pillow over my head to block out the sunlight. I tossed and turned but could not go to sleep. It made no sense to me. I was not thinking about church or what the preacher preached about that morning as I could not remember anything that was done or said by him or anyone. I just wanted to go to sleep, but something was keeping me awake. I got out of bed and looked through the house. No one was there. I had been left alone so that I could sleep. I looked out of the windows to see if anyone or anything was in the yard. The only thing in the yard was my truck. I did not understand it then, but the thing that was keeping me awake was something that could not be seen. It was God. When I realized this, I suddenly felt like I had murdered someone and hidden his body in the backyard, and the police were on the way. Then without a moment's hesitation that feeling left and was replaced by a comforting presence. It was like I knew what had to be done to make everything all right, and I was going to do it, whatever it was. I was not sure what it was, but I knew I was going to do it.

I often go back to that memory when I consider myself a failure and a vile offender against everything that the Bible teaches about church, Jesus, and what Christians are supposed to be. It is my only hope to go back to that church altar where I found myself that afternoon with no congregation watching, no invitational hymn playing in the background; only a faithful pastor sharing God's plan of salvation. I revisit the black waters of the river I was later baptized in on a cold November afternoon. I recall the old hymn being sung as I and twelve other people waded from the sandy shoreline into that cold water. It is the most precious memory of my life. There is no other event in my life that holds such an important place in my memory. None. There is no other moment in my life in which I felt such peace and purpose in life. None. There is no doubt in my heart or mind what happened to me that Sunday afternoon. I was saved.

I was twenty-one years old that November afternoon, and I cried like a baby. I really didn't know what this was that pulled on my entire being. I had never felt anything like this. All I knew was that when I left church that Sunday afternoon, something was eternally different about me. I would never forget what had happened that afternoon nor doubt its importance. Never.

The following weeks and months brought uneasiness. At a time when I thought everything had been squared between God and me, something was troubling me more and more. I had learned a lot in Sunday school classes. I listened to older Christians pray and was able to say grace at home, but still something was not quite right, and I did not understand what it could be. I did not know if God wanted something more of me, or if I wanted something more of God. It was something that I had to figure out.

I visited a Holiness church that was in revival one week. I went every night, and every night I did as the evangelist requested. I wanted to be saved, sanctified, and filled with the Holy Ghost. It was the memories of those faithful women at that small church of my childhood that sent me in search of something more. I had accepted Christ, quit smoking, and stopped doing anything that was labeled sin. I had prayed and fasted and was ready for the anointing of the Holy Ghost. It did not happen. No matter how long I stayed at the altar or how much I prayed, it just would not happen. I never spoke in tongues, and I never was compelled to shout. I enjoyed the sermons and the music, but the mystery of this anointing would remain a mystery to me. Men and women I greatly respected had this experience almost on a weekly basis. I could not understand why I was not afforded this gift. This anointing was the wonderful evidence that God's Holy Spirit had so filled your life that you spoke in an unknown tongue. I wanted this from God but it was not to be.

Then one Sunday morning as the pastor delivered his message, I pictured myself preaching. The seconds that passed brought with them a clear understanding of what had been troubling me. God wanted me to preach. It was like a storm that has passed over and moved on to reveal a clear sky. It was clear to me what God wanted. The same initial panic and paranoia that I had felt when under conviction by God's Holy Spirit for salvation was brief and replaced by a silent surrender of my heart. It was easy to make this silent submission to God. It was another thing to actually tell someone else.

There was no burning bush like Moses had, no blinding light that Paul met on the road to Damascus, no visions, voices, or even a penny laying heads up. It was just this undeniable feeling that I was called to preach, and all I had to do was say yes. I did.

I preached my first sermon on a Sunday night at my home church. It lasted forty-five minutes. People were yawning and staring at the ceiling. The pastor must have looked at his watch a dozen or more times. I don't know what I was thinking. The pastor would later tell me preaching a sermon is like flying an airplane; there comes a time when it is time to land.

I was a new Christian, and there was so much that I did not know about the Bible and living the Christian life. The things that

I needed to know could not be learned without some type of formal training. The pastor encouraged me to attend seminary training as soon as possible. It was very expensive to attend Bible college and the additional cost of moving and relocating to Nashville seemed like an impossible dream. The meager salary I earned as an EMT just barely paid the bills I already had. My dreams of attending seminary seemed just that—dreams.

Chapter V

"Forty Years in the Wilderness"

The first formal invitation I was given to preach was on Mother's Day.

The pastor had not realized this when extending the invitation, and he had put himself between a rock and a hard place, especially if I had another forty-five minute plane ride. But I had my mama to talk about, and if you get an old Southern boy talking about his mama, whatever comes out is going to be acceptable. It was a pleasant sermon as I recalled how my mother had taken care of my sister following a terrible Christmas season accident.

We lived in a house that to this day we still refer to as the rat house. It was across from the school I attended in the fourth grade. It was near Christmas, and my father was home from one his many trips to the veterans' hospital. He had not been drinking for a short time, and we were very happy. The house had earned the name "the rat house" because of the large rats that would invade our kitchen at night and drag whatever was on the table off onto the floor. Early Christmas eve morning we were awakened by two rats dragging a ham bone down the hallway. It was time for a rat killing. That afternoon several cousins and two of my uncles arrived with 22pistols, 4-10 shotguns, and a couple 12-gauge shotguns. They all had small shot loads and assembled in a circle outside around the pile of junk in the back field that had been there for years. Then my uncles poured gasoline on the pile, and everyone got ready. I don't believe they were ready for what happened next.

The fire burned slowly because my uncles had mixed oil with the gasoline to smoke out the rats. The smoke idea worked really well! Too well! Everyone had tears in their eyes when the rats started running from the pile. The shots started flying. People started hollering because several times the rats were not the only ones being shot. The shins and feet of many rat killers were blistered by the small shot. My uncles had been partaking of Christmas spirits, and they laughed and kept on shooting. My father did not join in. The idea of being around my uncles with loaded guns did not exactly appeal to him for some reason. I stood on the back porch with him, and watched this comical event come to an end as the dead rats were thrown onto the fire or onto an unsuspecting shooter. It was the funniest thing I had ever seen. Christmas morning was coming.

Christmas had come and gone and the last days of the holiday season were quickly passing. My sister had gotten up only a few minutes before my brothers and I and was standing in front of a space heater to warm herself. She had on a long cotton nightgown, and it caught on fire. Her screaming woke all of us, and we ran to see my father rolling her into a throw rug in the hallway. Flames leaped around his face and arms as he smothered the fire. My mother took my sister from my father, and he went to start the car. It did not start. It was a 1953 Plymouth and the icy ground made it impossible for him to push it. He ran for help. There were no ambulances so a relative took her to the hospital. She stayed there four months.

My sister had full thickness burns on the back of both legs from her ankles to her lower buttocks. The doctors were not sure that she would live through the first night in the hospital. She would not had lived if it had not been for the grace of God and the excellent nursing care she received.

My mother's oldest sister was a registered nurse, and she had devoted much of her time and livelihood caring for our family. She often brought food when there was no food and clothes when there were none. This might not seem saintly, but she had six children of her own. In these acts of compassion she did not just walk the walk, she ran it. She ran everything.

She guided my mother in the extensive care that my sister would require after she came home from the hospital. I was at recess at school when I saw my aunt's station wagon turn into our driveway. My classmates watched as they carried my sister inside. Everyone thought an ambulance had brought her because my aunt used her station wagon. While that scene remains clearly in mind, the most precious memories are those that no one saw.

In the afternoon and evening hours my mother had to give my sister bath soaks. It was still painful for my sister, but my mother would comfort her with hymns and prayers as she did what had to be done.

It would be the quiet hymns and prayers that echoed down the hallway of that old rat house that I shared on that Sunday morning's service. The successful service gave me courage to accept a second speaking engagement. This next speaking engagement revealed a whole new awareness of how people differ in religious beliefs and practice, even in the same denomination.

I traveled about fifty miles to a church that was built right in the middle of a field. On each side of the church were fields of tobacco. When I arrived, Sunday school had started so we just sat in the rear of the sanctuary and listened to the Sunday school teacher. We followed along in the literature and listened to each member insert his or her own interpretation of what the lesson's writer had written. I didn't say anything. I just sat and listened. The class was followed by an break period. Everyone got up and went outside, and the pastor invited me to join him outside.

I had noticed two huge cement birdbath-like things sitting by the entrance to the church. There was one on each side of the doorway. I did not know it at the time, but now I know what they were for. There were about ten or fifteen people gathered around each one, smoking. The piano player was smoking, the song leader was smoking, the pastor and his wife were smoking, the entire Sunday school class was outside offering up burnt offerings. I started smoking at about the age of fourteen and had quit when I joined the church. I always had heard from various sources that you could not be a Christian and smoke. But low and behold, right in front of God and everybody, the entire church was smoking. This business of being a Christian was not going to be so bad after all. I started to wade right on in among them but then I did not. I did, however, stop at the first store and bought a pack of cigarettes. The pastor had given me a twenty-five dollar check for that morning's service. It bounced higher than the smoke offerings I had seen at church that morning. The manager at the Piggly Wiggly store called me several times until I finally had to go pick up that check. The cigarettes were not the only thing that had left a bad taste in my mouth.

My experience as a Christian was in the babe stage. There were so many things that I did not know. The pastor lived several miles from the church area and made any effort to spend time with him difficult. I was asked to fill in for him one Sunday night. I had no experience in preparing a sermon. I had found out from a local pastor that there were parts to a sermon. There was an introduction, three points, and a conclusion, but other than that I knew absolutely nothing. Being under pressure with such short notice, I resorted to reviewing a Sunday school lesson and using it as an outline. I did not know any better. I was trying to not make a mistake and yet appear knowledgeable. I thought I did a very good job but was chastised in Sunday school the next week.

The chairman of the deacon board was the adult Sunday school teacher, and he had recognized the material. His comments were anything but encouraging and offered no instruction whatsoever. He would become the first of many Daddy Rabs I would encounter.

Daddy Rabs are men whose family members outnumber the rest of the congregation and have been at the church for the longest time. Therefore by their own appointment they are elevated to a position that rides herd on church business. They have a great say in the selection of a new pastor, but their most prominent position becomes apparent when it comes time to remove the current pastor. They always express themselves as God's chosen leaders for their church in this spiritual emergency. They become so absolutely possessed by their efforts to remove a pastor, it dominates every moment of their lives. If you see them at a barber shop getting a haircut, they speak openly about their position against the current pastor. Wherever they are, whatever they are doing, it includes their assessment of the current pastor's spirituality. Their chief object in life would be ridding the church of the current pastor; perhaps a man who only two years earlier had been promised to have been sent by God. They usually are the first to help unload the moving truck and the first to ask the pastor to get another one. Any battle or power struggle is never won by the pastor because the disharmony becomes so unpleasant for the church the church would simply fold to the man's position against the pastor. Many times this cycle of vicious power struggle starts over the simplest matter. The matters range from the color of carpet, to the building of Sunday school classes, to the selection of a new deacon. Sometimes it can even occur by accident, but mostly it occurs with intent.

I went and watched several pastors and evangelists preach wonderful sermons at revivals. They amazed me with their own personal ability to deliver these dynamic sermons. I studied the clothes they wore, the Bibles they used, their delivery of the subject matter. I studied everything about them. All were different men with different backgrounds and different styles of preaching from different denominations. It would be many years before I discovered the secret of their success. But I would learn the secrets of the mastery of the preach. Sadly when one achieves this the tender moments of uncertainty when one must rely totally on the Lord are replaced with a plan. Professional voices set in tone and tempo deliver sermons that have been delivered many times before. A sermon chosen for its past success finds its way into the week of revival. A pastor tells an evangelist about a current problem or situation and a sermon is pulled from the briefcase that deals with the current suggestion. I would find out that the truth of the matter was that older Christians liked to be entertained.

They have listened to so many preachers in their Christian lives that they will not settle for less. They expect great voices, great stories, and humor blended in the mix. They will tolerate a substandard message from a pastor every once in a while, but they will not listen to many. Too many and it would be time for this man to move on. Many times the sermons they think so poorly of are directed at helping them to make changes in their lives to be better Christians. They just do not feel the need to change. The only reasonable change that should be made is the pastor and his pitiful sermons. People do resist change. I know that I did.

This preaching business was starting to look not so good. People held you to a different standard, and I believed they should. There is no greater office than that of being a minister of the gospel. However, if you look at the greatest preachers in the Bible, they all were human; human beings that had problems being held to higher standards. Peter, who the Lord called the son of thunder, was rebuked by Paul. Paul and Barnabas had such a disagreement that they had to separate. They loved each other, but they just did not like what each other was doing very much. In this babe-in-Christ period of my life, the very last thing I needed were people expecting more of me than I could have possibly given. I could not have been a spiritual leader because I needed to be led, but I did not know that. I was waiting on orders from God. I read the Bible and prayed and knew the orders would be coming any minute. I had no doubt. All I had to do was wait. People around me were waiting to see this great commission I was to be off on. The longer no divine call came, the more people watched me. The more people watched me, the more I gave them to watch. There was no great falling away from the call into the ministry for me. It was more like the shot that was heard around the world.

It happened one Sunday afternoon as I was in the kitchen reading the Bible. I had been hunting the day before and had the shotgun leaning up in the corner of the closet. Out of my rear kitchen window I saw this rabbit run into a thicket behind my house. I had a small garden and rabbits were more than a nuisance. I reached for my shotgun and loaded it with what I believed was small shot. I took aim and shot into the thicket. I heard this horrible squealing. My hands started trembling. I thought I had shot a child. My heart raced as I ran to the wooded area. Expecting the worst, the squeals hushed and the thrashing in the brush ceased. I held my breath as I looked. There lying right in front of my eyes was my father in-law's prize sow, a Yorkshire pig. As she kicked her last kick and breathed her last breath, I felt a brief moment of relief. But then suddenly I realized what I had really done. There were few things he loved more than hunting and fishing, but this pig was at the top of that list. He was devastated.

The news of the swine homicide spread like wildfire throughout the small community. I noticed men looking at each other at the local gas station and laughing. I guess I would have laughed at something like that, but since I was the source of the story, I found its telling anything but pleasant. The sow had been butchered and smoked on the barbeque pit. This in itself was a community activity that spawned past and present homicidal swine stories as the pig cooked on the grill. Every story seemed to have one thing in common, a pig killer. Whether by vehicular homicide, death by drowning , or shooting by a crazed hunter, all pointed the finger at a crazed killer, a certified pig killer. That was me, a pig killer. It would literally take years for the memory of that bloody day to diminish to an annual event and there was a reason for that. The man that was the pig killer was not just a man, he was a preacher. He was a pig-killing preacher. Couple that with yet another bloody homicide and a man's chance for rehabilitation from the status of pig killer would require divine intervention.

It had been just a few weeks since the smoke from the barbeque pit filled that fall afternoon sky. Now the autumn air was filled with the cry of the deer hounds. One morning at the hunting club I was told it was safe for me to hunt because everyone had left their pigs at home. I simply ignored the many insults and enjoyed that afternoon's hunt. I had about five hounds that I had turned loose on a big deer track. Many hunters claimed that they could tell whether a deer was a buck or doe by the type of track it left on the dirt road it crossed. I never saw anyone who was able to do that. I just turned the hounds loose and listened to them trail and strike. When the deer was jumped and the hounds were in full cry, it was almost magical. It would take me back to the days of my childhood spent with my uncle and his fox hounds. I would find myself lost in the memories of yesterday and wishing my uncle could share this day with me. The day ended as it always does—with lost dogs. Whether they were curled up beside the comfort of a running brook or still chasing deer, who could say. The truth was it would be a long day waiting for any hound that was not caught by the last hunt. It was well after dark before I recovered the last dog and headed home.

The old Ford truck I was driving had only one headlight. I had never gotten it fixed because I drove it only on hunting days. I turned onto the blacktop road leading to my house. The light from the single headlight danced on the blacktop as I shifted gears. Then all of a sudden the road was full of black angus cows. There must have been seven in the roadway. I managed to miss most of them, but I could not miss them all. The right front of the truck struck one cow right in the head and killed it instantly. It also killed the only light that I had on the truck. So there I was. You can't make this stuff up.

The darkness of the night did not allow me to see who was herding the cattle from the roadway, but someone was. Then a car pulled up, and the driver drove on to his house and called the sheriff's department. But since it was a matter of a vehicular homicide and the cow still lay in the road, the sheriff's department sent the South Carolina highway patrol. People soon gathered at the accident scene. There was only one thing that got a rural community more stirred up than a pig killing, and that was a bovine homicide. Men were chewing tobacco and drinking Pepsi colas at the same time they were so worked up. The hunters who had CB radios began live news coverage that CNN would envy. It was a sight. I stood by myself looking at this huge black cow lying dead on this black roadway. I expected that at any minute these good old boys would drag out a piece of chalk and sketch the outline of the cow's body. I started thinking that I better call an attorney when the patrolman arrived.

He asked me basic traffic accident questions as he filled out his report. He also asked me if I knew who owned the cow and I replied, "Well, I guess it's the man who owns the fifty other cows on the other side of the fence." I was not trying to be smart or anything, I just thought it was common sense. I mean on one side of a fence you have one dead black cow and on the other side of that fence you have fifty or more live black cows. Well, there you go. The patrolman told me, "Look here, boy," as he spat his chew of tobacco, "if I needed a stupid answer I would have asked the cow if he knew who hit him, and that would be you wouldn't it, boy?" The crowd was silent trying to hear every word that was said. When they heard the patrolman's remark, they howled with laughter. There I was, a known pig killer, standing over a bovine corpse whose owner had to be summoned to the death scene for identification purposes. I could not believe that this was happening to me. The CB radios crackled with minute-by-minute updates as they developed. The man who owned the fifty cows on the other side of the fence arrived and walked over and looked at the cow. I expected him to be overcome with grief at the loss of such a fine cow, but he was not. He simply looked the patrolman right in the eye and said, "Nope, that is not my cow. I have never seen this cow before." My mouth fell open. I could not believe it! How could a man look at a dead black cow in the middle of the night and separate this cow from the herd of fifty or more black cows standing on the other side of the fence? It was beyond my understanding, and I said so. Even though there was not anyone else that owned cattle on that road, the patrolman asked me if I could prove that this man owned the cow. I had to reply that I could not and would not attempt to do so. If the man said it was not his then it certainly must not be his. I knew it was a no-win situation. The patrolman told me that if an owner could not be found, it was state law that the cow now belonged to me, and I had to get it off the highway. This sent the crowd into hysterical laughter, and they got in their trucks and left. The highway patrol officer also left, reminding me that I was responsible for the cow and to make sure no one else hit it. I was glad everyone had left because no one saw what a terrible time I had dragging that cow down the highway. The dogs barking in the dog box in the back of the truck and the cow leaving hide and hair on the highway were markings of a true bovine homicide for all to see and hear.

People and family had waited to see what great thing God was going to have me do. I was waiting for the denomination to license me to preach. You had to have been licensed for one year to preach under the watch care of your local church. At the end of that period, you were sent before an ordaining council to be examined by the council of elders, and then you could be ordained. Once ordained, you could pastor churches, baptize, conduct Communion services, and marry people. I had not yet been licensed. Being known as a pig and bovine killer does not lift one in the social standings of the community. In fact, it's hard to get people to listen to you preach when they already consider you a crazed killer. The truth for that community was that II was an outsider, and nothing would ever change that.

Nevertheless, the day came for me to appear before the ordaining council to be licensed. It was very brief, and they mostly talked about doctrines of their faith. They could have been speaking Greek as far as I was concerned because I didn't even know what a doctrine was. I just answered in the manner in which they prompted me, and then walked out with a piece of paper saying that I could preach. This brief interview would be the source of great controversy and mystery to me for many years.

The first year of my ministry was a wonderful year. The people of the church were special people. The church was in a growing phase. Me and the other new converts were hungry for spiritual things, and we were learning so much about the Bible. The choir had grown, and I was enjoying learning each part of the hymns. I paid attention to everything that was going on in the church. I wanted so badly to know how a church ran; like how the bills were paid and how the songs were chosen. I wanted to know it all.

The time passed so quickly. The months were full of special, wonderful services in which the Holy Spirit was so very real. These were not emotional events where fast and pumped up music pitched people into a frenzy of some kind. It was as if He was teaching me things that others had forgotten to teach me or chose not to. I shall always remember how tender the Lord lead me through this babe-in-Christ period. I was not only a babe in Christ, I was a preacher boy.

The title "preacher boy" was like a knock against your head. It was meant to remind you that there were a great many things that you had yet to learn. I had been learning the real meaning of love, the real meaning of everything. It was Christ. God's vast grace had provided the dearest companion who accompanied me every step of the way that first year. I am sure of that because I would not have made it to the second year without Him. It had been smooth sailing, but the storm clouds were gathering. Even a preacher could feel the cold winds of uncertainty bring a chill to our warm and friendly church.

It was at the conclusion of a Sunday morning service when the pastor announced his intention to resign from the church. He had been there twenty-one years, and he said he felt that it was time to move on. He said that he had not been looking for another church to pastor but felt that his ministry at this church was complete. The church was silent, quieter than I had ever heard it. Then slowly some of the older women started to sniffle. They loved this wonderful man who had shepherded them through births, deaths, and seasons of life as different as the seasons of weather. He had been the pillar of strength, the compassion of forgiveness, and the pastor we all believed God wanted us to have. Yet anyone could tell by his voice and his demeanor that he was not going to change his mind. Many attempted to sway his decision, but he just smiled and told them that he loved them and he knew they would want him to do what he believed God desired. His comforting pastoral effort seemed to soothe broken hearts for the moment, but the uncertainty scared everyone.

I've often thought about this, and what must have been in the pastor's heart and mind as he watched these people all but beg him to reconsider his decision. The church and pastor shared a knowledge of each-others truthful character. He knew which ones he could count on to be prayerful in this matter. He knew those who would make it their chief business to find out what happened to make the preacher want to leave. At a time like this there was a lot of gossip and rumors were everywhere. I guess the old saying was true after all. You can hear everything but the Lord's Prayer and meat frying. Even as he completed his four week notice he continued to remind everyone how the church should go about selecting another pastor. I don't think anybody was listening.

A Sunday afternoon luncheon was given for the pastor with gifts from many members. He and his family shared their thoughts about his twenty years of service and what it meant to them. Then he was gone. A pulpit committee was formed, and they were to seek possible candidates for the position. I was not included in any of this business. In fact, during choir practice that evening, as I entered the hallway leading to the choir loft, I heard the Daddy Rab inform the other members of the committee that I was not be asked to fill in during this period. He said that he thought this would only harm the effort. They laughed when one member said something that I was unable to overhear. All of a sudden I felt like the little boy standing at the lunch counter holding his free lunch ticket. Instead of a lunch ticket, I held a license to preach and these guys were determined that I would not use it at this church. I was devastated that these men who I attended church with would think that I would do anything to harm the church. I sure had no ambitions of being the church's pastor and knew that the next pastor would have to fill some pretty big shoes left by our former pastor. It was hard to look at these men's smiling faces during choir practice.

Men of all descriptions came and tried out for the pastoral position. They were tall, short, thin, and fat. Their styles of preaching were as vastly different as their appearance. Several business meetings were held following Sunday services to vote on a pastor. This went on for what seemed like forever. All through this process the Daddy Rab was in his glory. He contacted the preachers and would inform them of the church's decision. On Sundays when there was no preacher coming, a guest speaker was asked to fill in. The Daddy Rab was holding his ground on this issue. I would not be allowed to preach until the church had secured another pastor. I convinced myself that these men knew best and that this was an acceptable and wise decision. The church was in uncharted waters and emotions were running high after the loss of a beloved pastor. I cannot say that through all this my thoughts were always pleasing to the Lord.

I was at times angry. At other times I was confused when the Daddy Rab or others voiced their opinions about the men who were trying out for pastor. I asked myself who gave these men such rights as to intervene in what I considered God's business. After many months of searching for a pastor, the church decided to call one of the men who had tried out. He refused the offer, stating that he did not feel lead by the Holy Spirit to take the church. This pleased the Daddy Rab because he was not totally convinced this man was he right one. The church was running out of prospects. They had tried out so many men, and the church wanted this issue settled. I was not asked about anything related to the matter and simply cast my vote as other members did. I did not realize it at that time, but I was learning the most valuable lessons any minister could ever learn. I was seeing what a church goes through when selecting a pastor and that everything was not always as it appeared. What was apparent was a division that was developing between Daddy Rab's clan and the rest of the church body. All indications that this was coming to a head surfaced at one of the Sunday night business meetings.

The sanctuary was quiet as people filed into the church. I did not recognize all the faces that entered. I thought to myself it was a misfortune that we did not have a Sunday night service planned. I always liked the informal services that sometimes developed on Sunday nights as people appeared to have come desiring a blessing from the Lord. My desire was soon replaced by awe as I watched Daddy Rab lean across pews and greet people I did not know. He was smiling and waving at others like he knew them all his life. Come to find out he did. Their names were on the church roll, but they had not been attending church regularly for some time. He seemed in his glory. Then to my surprise, another group of people entered the church I also did not know. These people seemed to be seated near the group that opposed Daddy Rab's effort. His look toward these people told me everything that I needed to know. He greeted them, but his greeting was less than warm, and his eyes seemed to be darting around the church . He was counting votes. That man's ability to count those in church attendance on any given Sunday was phenomenal. His guess at the number present would never be off by more than ten or twelve. The number of people present grew by the minute. The piano player was playing a lively hymn, and the sound of the many gathered voices seemed to certify this night as a mighty fine night for a preacher calling, and so it was.

The Florida presidential election had nothing on this church when it came time for a preacher calling. The session began with a roll call of members present. Only two people in church that evening did not have their name called. These two were allowed to vote by Daddy Rab because his wife was the clerk and knew their names had simply been overlooked. No one questioned Mother Rab's authority as church mother of historical fact. She had written and underscored every major event of that church's history, and if she wrote it, well then it was true and that was all there was to that. Dates and names of events always bore her commentary as well as her famous ending quote, "And a good time was had by all." Yes, it was a fine evening for a preacher calling.

The meeting started out using Robert's Rules of Order but quickly entered into the loudest voice platform. The task of securing another pastor was wearing on the nerves of the congregation and it was showing. Daddy Rab was the moderator, and he had a great skill for using this position to direct his will during the meeting. His favorite device was to allow the most uneducated to speak as long as they chose. They would be allowed to ramble and quote Scripture as long as they desired. When they started talking about what Grandpapa or Mama used to say, someone in the congregation would call for a point of order. While these people rambled through their fifteen minutes of fame, Daddy Rab would look very interested and nod his head in sincerity. In this way he exhibited for all to see his fair and caring manner as moderator. His talent for closing a business meeting with nothing being accomplished was masterful. Somehow along the way he would always find a way to muster a tear and express his deep love for the church. People would leave the meeting dismayed that nothing had been accomplished. However, that night the church was having none of that. The church was voting on a preacher and every member seemed determined to settle this issue.

Each person stood and expressed his or her reason why this preacher should or should not be called as pastor. The preacher had preached the past two Sundays. I personally did not like his style of preaching, but I kept my thoughts to myself. He had told the church to decide on his effort before another speaker came because he did not believe in a personality contest. I had a certain amount of admiration for this statement. Daddy Rab on the other hand did not. A preacher who placed any kind of restriction on his ability to call another speaker did not sit well with him. The church had been praying for months about this pastoral selection and seemed determined to ignore Daddy Rab's suggestion for time to pray about it. A solution was reached when the church decided to dismiss the meeting and put off the vote until Wednesday night's service. He had done it again! I was amazed at his ability. He had gotten what he wanted, and the whole church seemed to believe that they had gotten what they wanted. This man should have been in professional politics. To tell you the truth, what occurred in that small rural town between Sunday night and Wednesday was nothing but true, polished, professional, politicking in the highest order.

The only thing missing during that week was bumper stickers. There were hundreds of phone calls, hundreds of handshakes, and several slices of homemade pound cake served with ice tea at afternoon prayer meetings held in various homes. The sense that this was an important event in the life of the church became more urgent and more passionate with each passing day. At stake was control of the church, and everyone seemed to know that but me. I thought it was God's church and that He should be in control of everything: our lives, our business, our homes, our future, and without question the affairs of His church. I had no idea that what would be voted on was the course of many lives. It was serious business.

Wednesday night came, and the voting membership displayed their desire by standing when casting a yes vote or a no vote. The yes votes won by a small margin. The church was almost split in their decision to call this man as pastor. Nevertheless, it had been voted on and all that was left to do was call him and inform him of the church's desire. I never knew if he asked what the vote was or if he was told. The expression on Daddy Rab's face told me that he might have lost this battle, but he had no intention of losing the war. Less than six months later the new minister and all those who voted for him would leave the church and start having church services in a house in town. I learned a lot about what a church goes through when they decide to call a minister. I don't know who was right and who was wrong or if anyone was. I do know that in my heart I was surprised by what I had seen and heard through this process. While this was a bittersweet learning experience, it was Preacher Calling 101. But I had not seen anything yet.

I can't explain what effect this had on my spiritual health. It did not lessen my desire to do what God wanted me to do, but it sure didn't do a lot to encourage me either. The end result was that I found myself less concerned about what the church did. It did not matter to me anymore. I attended church, but I was really confused about all this business. The tenderness of the heart had been replaced with something else. I was not sure what this something was but I was sure I preferred the former. It was not much different at work.

There was an innocence in being an ambulance driver. You don't know anything, but your efforts were always guided by compassion. In this emergency medical service business, your chief efforts seemed to be to do whatever it takes to survive from one shift to the next. The men and women who I worked with were becoming more callous with each passing day. I was too. I just did not recognize it, but I was changing. Ambulance drivers of yesterday were never so callous, but they were never asked to do the things the technicians were expected to do flawlessly. Paramedics were required to intubate patients in the most dire positions and places, readily assess patients, and treat according to protocol. For the emergency medical technician the training never stopped. Things had changed, and I knew it was not all for the good.

Things that used to happen at work that used to keep me up at night were now quickly forgotten. Types of injuries took on calloused names. People who had died in a fire were called crispy critters. People who shot themselves in the head were called people who had changed their minds. The calloused heart became a defensive barrier separating any troubling experience from our lives at home. What happened at work stayed at work, and if black humor helped us to achieve that goal we used it readily. The only problem with this protective measure was that it did not protect us from ourselves. We became different people without realizing it. Slow, minute changes were occurring in the way we thought, and it happened without us ever noticing. It took some time for me to realize that what was happening to me at work was also happening at home. I was becoming a different person, and I was not sure that I liked the type of person I was becoming.

I wasn't happy about anything anymore. The joy that I had received in my new Christian faith had been replaced with a cynical hardening of the heart. Everything was compared to the worst that I had seen or experienced most recently. People became whiners that had problems. Whether at church or at home, their problems were nothing compared to the people I saw in real life while at work. I was seeing people at the worst times in their lives, in moments in which they never expected anyone to know what they were doing, believing no one would ever know. But I knew. I knew things that never made the newspapers and things that if known would destroy lives, reputations, and even careers. Husbands, wives, mothers, fathers, cousins, brothers, sisters, sons, and daughters were guilty of immoral deeds that many times led to violence. I was seeing how dark the world really was and it became harder to find my way. Something had to be done. I had to do something to find a way out of this. The way led south, back home to Georgia.

The U-haul truck was loaded, and the family assembled for the farewell event. This event would be repeated many times in the years ahead as preaching directed the routes and seasons of travel. There were the usual well wishes and the questioning as to whether this was the right thing to do or not. I was not sure if this was the right thing to do at that time, but would realize later that it was the only choice. It's funny as men and women plot their life's course how often they forget to trust God with their direction and care. We often choose the wrong course and find ourselves out of God's will. It is up to Him to make us realize that. We are not supposed to be looking for signs or miracles that point us in that direction. We use our common sense and biblical principles to make these choices. If we do make a decision and truly believe it is the right one when in fact it is the wrong one, God will let us know. He will not only let us know but will provide the means by which we can correct the situation quickly.

The whining of the U-haul truck tires on the blacktop highway seemed to be humming a song as the white lines rolled by the window when we crossed the state line into Georgia. I could not help but reflect on the many memories that we were leaving behind. Some were so precious I would tuck them deeply within my heart and recall them during hard times. There were far more richer memories than poor ones. I remembered Mother Rab's saying as we crossed into Georgia and could not help but repeat it concerning all the memories, good and bad, "And a good time was had by all."

There is only one thing more real than the past you have just left behind and that is the future in front of you. I am almost convinced that the destination that awaits us is not as important as the going. It's the going that offers destinations that are abundant in the riches of life. It is there that you find happiness and character. People and preachers make a lot of plans about God's business, but it is usually the man passing by that God has chosen. I was not sure where we would end up, but I believed wherever it was it would be God's choosing and not mine. I could not have been more right.

Chapter VI

"Israel Must Have a King"

The weeks passed quickly after our arrival back in Georgia. Within three weeks I had started to work with the fire department as an emergency medical technician. The state requirements in Georgia were higher than in South Carolina, and I had to attend classes to assume an intermediate level. We found a church just three blocks from my mother's home. That church had been there for years, but I had never seen it or knew anything of it. I thought to myself how strange it was that God had to move me over three hundred miles to seek a church just three blocks from where I had spent most of my life. The pastor was a wonderful man of God who loved the church and the ministry.

His life had been devoted to pastoring churches, and he had a doctor of divinity degree. His ability to communicate with any type of person was masterful. His heart was pure, and I admired and respected this man and knew I always would. It would be under his pastorate as his associate pastor that he would instill within me the hunger for truthfulness with God. Above all things a sincere and honest heart that sought God's leadership would be successful in any task. Many months later I would leave the church headed for seminary. I did not understand why it was so important that I go. He had taught me so much about Scripture and the art of preaching, sermon preparation, pastoral duties, and so much about loving people. I could not imagine what else there was to learn.

Now I know that it was not the biblical education I would attain that would make my ministry successful, but it would be the acceptance of other preachers, deacons, and church members who had graduated from the college. It would be the evidence of a preacher boy's effort of preparation for the task that lay ahead.

College was a struggle from day one. I worked three part-time jobs in order to support my family and attend college. It was a religious paradox . The living of the Christian life while at college was so vastly different than at home. For example, men and women swimming together was forbidden at college and at youth camps sponsored by any association. However, local churches sponsored and developed such activities away from college. There were several such winks of tolerance. There was a guided effort to summon the student to realize there must be a separation from the secular world . It was scriptural and helped develop a conscious awareness of what one was allowing in his or her own life. The college was full of wonderful Godly men and women who had dedicated their lives to the Lord's service. Missionaries often came and presented programs which showed the efforts of evangelism in many parts of the world. These people had given their entire lives to the evangelistic effort. The college was indeed a place of preparation for such men and women who would become educators, evangelists, missionaries, and pastors. For me it was the biggest disappointment of my life, and at that time I believed it to be the greatest failure of my life.

The jobs I was working were on scattered shifts. In the morning it was pre- requisite classes and in the early afternoon I was a handyman for a rich couple who ran a classic arts business out of their home. They pronounced my name wrong and always used a nasal tone when speaking to me. The man would call me in from cutting grass to replace a light bulb when he could have done so in less time than it took to walk to the door and summon me. I considered this a lesson in Humility 101. His Mercedes had to be washed every day. His lawn had to be cut every other day. His furniture had to be moved out of the sunlight and then replaced when the afternoon light changed. He and his wife both shared great delight in ordering this to be done and that to be done. It seemed at times that the useless tasks that I was assigned were a contest between them to see what the other could get the hired help to do. I did not know their beliefs, but it was obvious that they thought little of the Christian faith. I considered my Christian testimony would best be illustrated by completing each task with humility and done to the best of my ability. The difference between my former occupation and this job's requirements was so vastly different. I had to keep reminding myself that I did not have to be a handyman if I did not want to be. I was preparing myself to be able to tell people about heaven, but I was not prepared for the hell I would have to go through in order to do so.

Completing the afternoon lesson in humility I would then attend a class, eat lunch with my family, and then be off to sack groceries for four hours. I would then eat supper and study quickly for classes the next day and get to bed early. I had to be at UPS to load trucks at one in the morning. This was only a three-hour job, but I don't know how a man could last longer than this working at the pace these people required. The foremen would stand at the back door of the truck and curse and scream every minute while you worked. They wanted you to work like you were pulling children from a burning house, gripping each package and cramming it tightly in the trailer. They did not want an inch of space wasted in the cargo area. Packages never stopped coming down the feeder bands nor did the insults. At the peak of their ranting and raving I would simply reply, "Shaking the bush boss, shaking the bush." I would always leave this part of the day physically drained saying that was the last day. Tired and wet from sweat, I would drive home for a shower and a quick nap before I had to do it all over again. Each morning I prayed for strength and courage to keep from quitting. But it would require more than courage. It would require more money.

The reality of trying to attend college while supporting a family was getting more real every day. A young mother suddenly found herself alone in a small apartment with two small children. I was never there. The basic courses I was taking were required but did little to achieve a sense of accomplishment. Later in life I completed my college education and received a degree in nursing and Bible studies, but at that time it was impossible. It was time to go. It was sad and I felt like the greatest failure in the world.

Within a short time I was back at work for the fire department and was attending the church I had attended prior to attempting college. It was not too long before I was called and asked to try out at a church. I remember the first time I heard this term used. It sounded like I was trying out for some kind of team sport. The term proved to be worthy of the similarity.

The week before the try out flew by with each day bringing a heightened sense of awareness that my life was about to change. The church was located in south Georgia in a rural farm area. That is like saying water is wet. The entire southern part of Georgia is some kind of farm community. The drive down was a test of faith in itself. The automobile I was driving had "may pop" tires, and the motor was subject to running hot. The road lead through rolling fields of peanuts and huge pecan orchids. Corn, cotton, and soybean fields suggested plant rotations. The children were amazed by the size of these fields. In their small lives nothing could have seemed more grand than the beauty of the green rows neatly separated by the plowed red Georgia clay.

The early Sunday morning air was blowing through the windows of the car. There was a freshness in the air and a freshness stirred within all our thoughts. The excitement bubbled within my heart and the possibility that the day may offer caused my palms to sweat. This was over thirty years ago and tears still moisten my eyes when

I remember that morning. The little blue Chevrolet Nova rumbled down the two lane country road as God's caring hand kept the tires from blowing out.

My Bible lay on the front seat with an outline of the morning's sermon. It was not a sermon I had preached before, and I had spent a great deal of time on its preparation. Sermons are developed over time and requires a measure of patience and meditation. It is not like every time you open your mouth a divine utterance from the throne of God will resonate throughout the sanctuary . Some preachers believe that when they stand behind a pulpit anything they say is divinely inspired.

The unexplainable confidence of knowing that you have chosen the right text, the right message, at the right time, still baffles me. But when it happens, the Spirit of God seems to make everything perfect. When a man allows God to have His way in the preparation and presentation, one could expect the unexpected. Paul called it the foolishness of preaching, but he above all others knew that God spoke to human beings through His word. He knew that if men submitted themselves wholly to God's will someone in need would hear the answers to questions within his or her heart. Humanity could find its way back to God's grace, if men obeyed the Lord's leadership. Preaching was an art of mastering language, speech, and gesture. Preaching was style, delivery, and tempo. More importantly, it was and will always be the right message, at the right time, at the right place. That morning I felt a fresh hunger within my soul to preach, to tell people the good news of this gospel and what it meant to them as individuals, as a family, and as a church. What He had done for others He could and surely would do the same for them.

The church was nestled in a oak grove. The giant oaks surrounded the church and their shadows rested on its roof. There was a large graveyard beside the road and a dirt driveway that wound its way back to the church. It was nine forty-five in the morning and already the church yard was a buzz of activity. Men and women were hurrying inside the fellowship hall carrying pots and trays of food. They glanced over their shoulders in our direction as they disappeared into the small brick building.

The church was built around the end of the Civil War, and rested on the original foundation even though remodeling efforts had been done throughout the years. The sanctuary seated around 150 and the Sunday school classes were separated from the main sanctuary by sliding vinyl curtains. The wooden floor and wooden pews bore the weathered character of a country church. Each church had its own character, and through its appearance that character can be seen and realized. To me this church expressed an old fashioned gospel that had survived the seasons that came its way and yet still thrived. Its well-traveled floor and concrete steps bare of the paint once applied spoke of a path that people remembered and returned to often. The graveyard was well kept and the old graves stood as senior statesmen. Moss hung from the oaks and the spring breeze caused them to sway, almost beckoning a friendly welcome to us as we got out of the car. This old church was so beautiful to me. Something stirred so deeply within my soul that there was no doubt this was not a trial sermon but instead a homecoming.

We took our seats in the church and received several nods of acknowledgement but no official welcome. The Sunday school hour began with a short red-haired man walking up to the pulpit and ringing a bell. Several children were herded behind the curtains, and they were pulled closed. The red-haired man pulled a wooden stand in the isle between the pews and began his lesson. He was a man of gestures as he waved his hands and raised his voice while making points he considered important. His Southern drawl at first seemed awkward but immediately blended in with the comments of the class. I looked around the church and saw several elderly ladies. They were all dressed in their Sunday best and sat quietly paying attention to the teacher. Out of the corner of my eye I could feel their glances, and if I acknowledged one of them they would simply smile and nod. With these frequent acknowledgements, the hour slowly passed by. The lesson was concluded and the preacher again rang the bell and instantly the church began filling with entire families. I had no idea where all these people came from, but suddenly the sanctuary was full of people. The Sunday school report was given and just as quickly as it had began the hour was over.

It was 10:45 and the worship hour was to begin at eleven o'clock. In those fifteen minutes occured the traditions that must have been carried on in rural churches for many years. It was a time of social activity rivaled only by the local pecan festival. Voices and laughter filled the air as people greeted one another and caught up on the latest news. Children ran in and out of the church hindered only by the occasional tap on their behinds each mother offered as a token of social acceptance. I don't think any child realized they had been to church if they didn't go home with Georgia clay on their clothes and at least one tap on their bottom. It was as normal a Sunday as sweet tea and fried chicken at dinner. It was great.

The service was everything I prayed for. The songs were perfect. Every pew was full of people. I was so nervous that I could barely breathe. I sat in the pastor's chair and wrestled with myself as to how one is supposed to sit. There were so many people watching my every move. My palms were sweaty and my pulse raced. But somehow it all seemed too grand.

The Holy Spirit has always been a pleasant surprise to me. He seems to be at His very best when we're at our very worst. His ability to take our modest efforts and open an avenue of thought which illustrates a point is truly amazing grace in its finest hour. I suddenly found myself saying things that I never intended to say and receiving such attention and reception. I believe that's the beautiful mystery of God's Holy Spirit. He does indeed move in mysterious ways. I've said some things in sermons and had no knowledge of their piercing effect on men's hearts and minds. A sermon requires two things. It must be intellectually understood by the mind and received by faith in the soul. The eternal soul of man is in his heart. What it binds here on earth is bound in heaven. What a person's dreams and desires are will not change simply because he finds himself one day standing before a Holy God. It is what it is. But in that hour of worship service, everything seemed to point to a direction long ago chosen, not by me or the congregation but by God's divine will.

Chapter VII

"Just As I Am"

The sermon was completed ten minutes before twelve noon. This was the quitting time in the field of preaching. Ten minutes of invitation afforded any and all the proper time to set eternity in order. Or at least that was what many churches believed. The people expected to walk out of church at twelve noon and not five or ten minutes later. If you extended the period, you had more people watching their watches than you and listening to their bellies rather than what you had to say. I still remember my very first sermon that lasted an hour. Afterward the pastor told me preaching was like flying a plane, you had to land it. I just kept flying in circles above the airport. I did not know it then, but I knew it now and one should be prepared and able to do just that; land the plane. Land the plane at the right destination with the delivery made on time and in proper order. The demands of doing this seemed wrong at first, but over time I could see its proper restriction, especially after hearing many different preachers. Some men would stand behind the pulpit and then, like a cannon being fired, would explode a series of verbal volleys that would leave you expecting them to pass out from hypoxia.

Like a hound in full cry, they would bellow with their baritone voices shaking the windows in the church and scaring the babies awake from their naps. There was no building up to an important climax or introducing a topic of importance, just a hollering of well-practiced religious terms that were ingrained in their makeup. One might say, "Bless God." He used this term in the worst sense. "Mama died. Bless God." "The house burned down but bless God!" I was amazed by how many years these men had done that. Generations of congregations had grown up expecting the next pastor to preach in the same manner. If he did not, well, he was not the preacher brother Bob was. On the other end of the spectrum were these defined soft-spoken men who preferred poems and rolling vowels. Men who stood like cast stone and let silence be their scream for repentance. What was amazing to me was that God used every one of them.

In the area of preaching, men came from every walk of life. Some had very successful efforts and others would always seem to struggle. Whatever their past , experience, or training, it did not seem to matter. When it came to the moment the sermon ended and the invitation was being given, something happened then. Man's efforts were over, and the Holy Spirit spoke to souls. It did not matter ,and more often than not, the preacher would never know what he said that registered in the congregation's spiritual awareness. That was God's business. Men would gage their efforts by the number that came down the aisle, raised a hand, or were baptized. The truth of the matter was only a divine God knows what happens within the hearts of men and women who sat under the sound of the preached gospel. The invitational hymn was announced to the congregation. The musicians and song leader assumed their roles as this dramatic scene unfolds. A scene in which I believe angels stand in awe of.

It is the moment one cannot deny when it happens. It is the sudden awareness of another existence, a real conscious awareness of one's own soul. When someone once asked me to explain this moment, I referred them to this comparison. Picture a baby supported by a mother in a tub of bath water. The water's depth is sufficient to cover the head. Should the mother release the child and its head be covered by the water, the baby would begin to frantically move both legs and arms in an effort to survive. The baby cannot explain why it needs to breathe. It cannot explain why it must survive, but it will expend any amount of effort just to live. The eternal soul of man cannot explain its need to respond when summoned by God's Holy Spirit, but yet it knows it must. It is only the soul beckoned by the Spirit of God that can acknowledge this event. There is no troubled conscience, no battle between the ego and id, no philosophy, no awaking mores. This is a connection from the other side, the spiritual world, the place where God is. The place where Jesus is. The place where the Holy Spirit of God radiates throughout eternity traveling at the speed of thought. It is the moment of spiritual reckoning for the souls of humanity. But it can also be the moments where horrible mistakes are made.

I recall at a baptismal service where several were to be baptized, a most unforgettable candidate. She came down into the pool of water wearing rather tight khaki pants and a white blouse. After receiving the ordinance charge of baptism and being submerged under water, she came up out of the water wiping her face with a towel she had been handed. Nothing unusual. In fact quite expected, but no one expected her exit from the water to be so memorable.

As she stood in the middle between myself and an older deacon who assisted me, this young lady began running her fingers through her long blond hair. As she did this, she smiled at the congregation as if she was filming a commercial for shampoo. She then walked up the three small steps leading out of the pool, but as she did she continued to run her fingers through her hair while smiling at the congregation. The thin wet khaki pants and white blouse were partially draped by the towel, but the young woman's stride up those steps reminded me of Marilyn Monroe's performance of "Happy Birthday" for JFK. At the top of the steps, she stopped, turned toward the congregation, waved, and said, "Wooo...wee, I mean O' hal...leeee...luu...ya!" She then ran her fingers through her hair and exited the baptism area. The old deacon in the pool looked at me and said, "I don't believe that took, do you preacher?"

The young lady had been pressured by her new mother-in-law to make a decision for Christ. It became the center of family concern and constant attention by the mother-in-law and the girl's husband. She had come from a Christian home, but her family had left one's decision of faith a personal matter, and so it was. The young husband somehow considered her following him immediately in accepting Christ and joining the church as part of the marital vow. So he and his mother had applied every tactic short of tasing to bring this girl to her knees. She finally had made a decision to do something to get them off her back, and her behavior during the baptismal service was her public statement of belief. Nothing more, nothing less.

A public expression of faith should be evidenced by a changed life. Mothers stand silent, and their joyful souls weep as a wayward child walks toward an altar. Wives have trembled as a hard-hearted husband accepts Christ before everyone in the church. It is the gospel in its finest hour.

The hymn "Just As I Am" was written by a slave runner who was saved, and I believe the words portray one of the truest truths of the gospel. We are what we are. Nothing more and nothing less. Sinners. God's grace, for some unexplained reason, affords a brief summoning from heaven. Think of that. From the very being of God, His Spirit summons man's attention to reckon the condition and fate of his eternal soul. There is no denying that fact. Whether he acknowledges this at that moment and accepts God's forgiveness or not, it does not change the fact that this event occurred. He cannot deny that he feels His Spirit in his quickening mortal soul. It is more than an emotion, more than any sense of duty or acceptance. It is something he has never felt before in his life. It is God speaking to him for the first time in his conscious mind. Sometimes the Lord's beckoning to his soul might go on for days before he acknowledges God's Spirit. Many times people know this is going to happen before they dress themselves for church. The stories of grace are as vastly different as the faces of the people who find themselves at the throne of grace. There are far too many who refuse such an acknowledgement.

The invitation was given and Uncle Eli stood with the rest of the congregation. The people that watched him knew he was a troubled man. He grasped the back of the pew in front of him and held on tightly. He stared down at the floor never acknowledging what was going on around him. The hymn was completed and the invitation closed. In spite of the preacher's plea for any to come forward, he did not. Instead he went outside the church and sat under a large oak tree and smoked. That was where his wife found him. Dead. Sitting. His face purple and vomit on his shirt. Cigarette still burning in his hand. He simply went the wrong way during the invitational hymn. A deacon told me the story of Eli as we looked at the base of the tree where he had sat. I could not help but hear the hopelessness in his voice. He had loved this man and learned much about farming from him. He was Eli's nephew.

Eli had been a man's man to all his young nephews and was respected by all who knew him. Regardless of all that this man had said and done in his life that was good and proper, his final choice was wrong. Those who loved him, those who had prayed for him, and those who watched him believed he went the wrong way. No one really knows what happened under that oak tree. No one but God and Eli know what was said or what was promised . That is the amazing grace of God. It rests between the soul of man and God. It cannot be measured in the number of stanzas of a hymn, or the minutes of an invitation, or the place of death. It basks in the riches of God's grace found in Christ. It is not up to any preacher or well-wishing loved one to place the departed anywhere but in the hands of a good God. He will do what's right. That is a certainty beyond our ability to comprehend. In fact it is hard to understand all that happens when it comes to the measure of grace afforded to man. It is hard to understand a lot of things that happen in this life. Who lives. Who dies. Who has ten fingers and ten toes. Who sees beauty and hears the beautiful sounds of this world and who stumbles and wrestles with darkness every day of their lives. I believe it is equally impossible to know and understand the workings of grace. Was it truly God's choice long before the world began who would be saved and who would not? Was it that God knew who would believe and who would not? Was it possible to accept the invitation of grace and truly be saved and then fall from that grace? From questions like these came many denominations and beliefs.

Many have their own ideas about what certain doctrines mean. I have summoned my soul many times in search of answers to these questions. I have found merit in many such issues relating to doctrine but have failed to see the merit of importance many place on them. For what does it matter when it's your time to sit under the oak tree.

This first invitation proved to be typical of the many that would follow. As the invitation hymn was sung, young men and women came forward. They would be baptized in the following weeks to come. Now the die was cast. I was hooked and, the rush of God's Spirit moving so openly in the church was awesome. I believed it would always be that way, but this was just a trial sermon and there was a lot yet to be decided . Serious decisions were to be made in the next two hours and much would have to be prayed about. But of equal importance in prayer effort was the closing benediction and blessing on the food.

Chapter VIII

"Manna from Heaven"

There was something just as spiritual and meaningful to Southern church folks as a good sermon or gospel singing, and that was dinner on the grounds. Deciding what to eat was not a favor afforded to a visiting minister or current pastor. You had to sample a little of everything that was spread out. Outside tables were iron and weather worn, but each was draped with the whitest tablecloths. White and decorated cloths covered each tray of food. The women of the church and visiting churches stood behind their preparations and smiled as the people chose their meals. It was for some women the finest hour of womanhood. Beautiful smiles and warm gestures for one to take a larger portion or an extra spoonful replaced for many widows an opportunity to prepare these huge meals they were famous for. Again and again the scene had been repeated over the years, but time had not weathered or worn the Southern ladies with their pleasantries at such a time. Mrs. Daddy Rab would have said, "A good time was had by all."

I can still remember the pleasure from passing by all the tables and bidding remarks to everyone. The atmosphere was relaxed, and everyone was talking and laughing. The people seemed excited about the future and what had just happened in the church service. The former pastor, who had been there almost thirty years, had died and that morning's service convinced many that God had not left with the former pastor. His wife was there, however, and her presence somehow told the church folk that it was all right that the church continue. She was a darling of a pastor's wife. Her white hair lay perfectly on her neck, and her eyes retained the sparkle of her youth. She was most kind and supportive with comments that were heard clearly and loudly by those around. I watched her that afternoon, and once I saw her sitting there gazing off in the cemetery. I wondered what she might have been thinking or what emotions ran through her. Her dress was smartly stylish, and I noticed the women watching her. She must have won their hearts many years ago. I had only seen her a couple of hours ago and yet I felt as if I had known her forever. But that was the way it was with everyone there.

I don't know if it was a gift that I was given, but I was always able to read people very well. While I was no walking lie detector, my first impressions were usually right. After all these years, I can't really remember being surprised by people. Morals were a whole different matter, however. Moral failure, whether gross in nature or social acceptance, did not occur because of weakened morals. It happened because of the power of sin in someone's life. The inherent nature of fallen mankind is a result of rebellious sin. Weakened morals are simply overpowered by the strength of sin. There is no greater influence in the physical world than sin. God must have thought so. That's why He sent His Son Christ Jesus.

I could feel all eyes on me as I passed from family to family. The conversations were brief and cordial as I made small comments which suggested I indeed was paying attention. The art of conversation is a natural gift for some people while others struggle mightily with it. As a minister you must be able to carry on a conversation in the most awkward moments while convincing the listener the conversation is meaningful and without effort. Southern people love talking but at their own chosen speed. Why, it would be rude and uncivilized for one to appear to be rushing another while in verbal discourse. I've always heard one had to be a good listener, but being in control of a conversation is far better. Proactively speaking is more than not allowing another to get a word in edgewise. It is directing attention, attitude, and common interest. Dinner on the grounds was the setting where one could view these common Southern verbal courtesies. These courtesies directed the path of conversation from one end of the dictionary to the other, from one topic to another with such ease one would ask the other, "What were we talking about?"

Talking, talking, and more taking. Southerners love it. People will ask, "How did we get on that subject anyway?" The truth is they wanted to talk about it all along, it just took a few minutes to get there. An excellent conversationalist will remove the "few minutes to get there" and actually have the other person introduce the preferred discourse. Saying what you want said, talking about what you want to talk about, does not always mean you have to be the one doing all the talking. Courtesy is more than Southern hospitality. Courtesy is the art of conversation, and any true art form cannot be rushed. Such was this lazy Sunday afternoon affair. The food had been eaten, introductions made, and it was a perfect end to a perfect morning. God was great and God was good, but now I had to have my first meeting with a deacon board as a pastoral candidate. I was not sure how well that would turn out.

The chairman of the deacon board was a big man. He had been a Marine, and he carried himself with an air of confidence. He was very pleasant and smiled a lot. Everyone liked him, and his wife's father had served many years on the board until his death. I liked this man. He had been the person who contacted me regarding coming down for this trial sermon. I walked up the stairs, and we sat down in one of the Sunday school rooms. There were three other deacons there. The redheaded man who had taught Sunday school and led the singing was there as well as another man who was nondescript. By that I mean he really did not stand out in any fashion at that time. He seemed pleasant and spoke highly of the church membership and the church's history. The fourth man was short with premature graying hair. His voice was gruff, and he spoke in short sentences. There was something about this man, but I really was not sure what it was. He was friendly and seemed very interested in my answers. This experience was new for all the deacons and myself. They had had a pastor for almost thirty years. While I'm sure they had decided weighty matters of church business before, this was new ground for all.

The scene should have been painted. There are few moments in a man's life where such things happen. In this business where eternal souls were at stake, and the course of the church was to be set, someone should have taken note of such a historic moment. We all believed God was doing so and set about this business in the best fashion we could. When each man on the board spoke, he spoke in the clearest voice he could muster and chose his words carefully. When one of them seemed to be pondering if what he said was right or in line with the others' thoughts, another would voice agreement. They were trying really hard to make this comfortable for everyone. They were trying to be sincere in their duties and guarding against any error. I was so relaxed with these men and sought God's will and presence. It was a very emotional moment for me. I could remember Daddy Rab's deeds and the lonely months of isolation I had felt as young preacher boy. I could feel the uncertainty, but I could feel the faith. God's presence was more real there in that moment than He had been during the service. I could barely contain the tears. My heart already knew that this church would call me as pastor. I already knew that this was my responsibility even before it became a reality. I believe these men felt this as well. Their attention and eyes said it all. Nothing distracted them from their thoughts. Like vascular surgeons exploring a leaking suture line, these men were searching each other's thoughts for any questions they might have missed. As the meeting concluded, money was discussed. The salary was two hundred dollars a week. The church would also furnish a place to stay. Where that would be was not yet known because the church had never needed a parsonage. They would find something to rent. Neither myself or the deacons acknowledged our spiritual gut feeling. We promised each other to be in prayer concerning all we had talked about, and the church would decide. I only asked them to decide before calling someone else. I had remembered that and always respected the minister who said it. It was God's business. No contest.

The phone rang that Wednesday evening as I was sitting on the front porch swing. The sun was going down so it must have been around 8:30. The board would have had time to have the Wednesday night prayer meeting and then get right on into the preacher calling business. I remembered Daddy Rab's efforts, and I wondered who the Daddy Rab was or if there even was one at this church. I was scared I guess wondering about my job with the fire department. They had re-hired me when I returned from Bible college, but there was no promise of that happening again. The city council had accepted the county EMS into the fire department and not everyone saw the need for that. The firemen were paid less than the EMTs, and they resented that. The EMS folk resented not receiving state fire benefits. This concept was conceived in the California and New York fire departments, but down in Georgia it was like mixing oil and water at the time.

The EMTs and firemen liked each other, and some were really good friends. The friendship was strained when a fireman tried to tell an EMT what to do or an EMT tried to tell a fireman what to do. They had been separate services for so long and professional jealously clouded many issues. Most firemen were Godly men, but as in much of life, some were not.

I had a fire officer who made quite a bit of sport of me by saying that the sisters better watch out because I would walk up to them and stick the Holy Ghost slap through them. His remarks were crude and offered only when he thought he had an appreciative crowd. The daily chores around the station were supposed to be shared equally, and for the most part they were. But the number of responses EMS made they were not. When EMS had finished the busy part of the day and returned to the station, their house duties would be waiting for them. Sometimes a friendly fireman would help out but then faced the risk of being assigned that duty for a week. Night would fall and there would be no non-emergency transfers but only emergency responses.

The city EMS was now covering the county as well, and the call volume was exceeding the ability of staffed ambulances to handle. The EMS was responsible for drowning and rescue calls. A truck had been designated for these calls, but only EMS personnel drove it. EMS and fire departments were still figuring things out then. The equipment and procedures were being developed with fire department standards across America. But here in the South the good ole boy seemed to circumvent real progress. In the years to come, this EMS department would be one to envy, but now it was the redheaded stepchild. It would take many years for that to happen. Nevertheless, I was an ambulance driver, and the thought of leaving something that I loved to do was very sobering. I could hear the telephone ringing in the distance, and I suddenly realized the ringing was bringing the time for a decision a lot closer. I began asking myself a thousand questions.

Have I really prayed about this thing? Is this really what God wants me to do? What about the well-being of my family? What in the world am I supposed to do? All these questions were futile. The decision had been made a long time ago and not by me. For some reason, God had chosen me for this beginning and a beginning it was. There would be so many firsts I would never remember them all. Each challenged and some demoralized. Nevertheless, it was decided by God, that I was sure of. I'm even more sure of it now. But things are not always clearly seen in the fog of battle.

Many times people have sought counsel about a decision they had to make in their lives. Some decisions are silly and some are gravely important. People have said there is no such thing as a stupid question. Well, yes there is. I remember a preacher friend of mine telling a youth campers about the night he had to make a decision about a church. He said he walked into the headlights of his truck to open a gate, and there in front of him lay a huge green frog. He said, "Lord, if you want me to do this, make the frog jump that way, or if you want me to do that, make the frog jump that way." *I don't believe I would have told that,* I thought to myself, but I've heard a lot said that I would not have said. Doing what God wants you to do is not always so easy.

It is no big secret, however, to know exactly what God wants. First of all, God would never ask you to do something that is contrary to His Word. The Bible teaches what a person is to do when faced with certain circumstances. It is no secret and it is not easy either. The second thing is that God would never ask you to do something that would destroy your family. God is a family God. He chose certain families and still does today. Families are very important to God and He places a great deal on the family's integrity. The third aspect of finding out what God wants is the measure of faith. God always asks for faith expressions. There are no sure things, no promises of success, or finish lines in sight. You must just believe that He will enable you to accomplish whatever it is. Lastly, He will accomplish the job you are sent to do. There will be no defeat. Accomplishing what God would have you do will not always meet man's acknowledgement of success. But no man will be able to find failure when God sends His servant to do a job. Many will stand with their mouths open wondering how you were able to do that. It might be days, weeks, or even decades before accomplishments may be measured or realized, but they will one day be acknowledged. God never asks someone to do something He doesn't intend for you to accomplish. You must believe that beyond and above everything else. I did.

The sun cast moving shadows on the front porch floor as I sat swinging. The day was ending, but before it did, it would require a decision. Many evenings I had sat with my brothers and sister around Mother on the front porch seeking the familiarity and safety of her words. I searched within my own heart for that comfort. I already believed in my heart that this church was going to ask me to be their pastor, and I needed to have this settled beyond a doubt. I had chosen one career based on the first sight of that bright red ambulance, and I was about to choose another after seeing only one church. The phone rang.

The man's voice was as pleasant as before when we had spoken. He said the church had voted that night, and the vote was unanimous to call me as pastor. I was so excited. I was so scared. The fact that the church vote was such a solid vote implied unity. Unity is very important and without it a church suffers. I had seen that in my early preacher boy days. The fact was that I was still a preacher boy, but this was taking the first step to becoming a man of God. A man of God. What a humbling declaration for a mere human being to assume. To me it means perfection of God's grace in your life. It means to be like Moses, David, and the apostle Paul; men whose lives not only changed their course but the course of the whole world. The offices of the church are select in purpose and direction. All intend to serve God's purpose and promote the gospel message throughout a world so vast in diversity and geography. The footprint that a man is required to make might weather in a neighborhood or on a missionary field on the other side of the world. But the office of pastor is one of a familiar culture with an endearing love, measured in patience, forgiveness, endurance, and faith. To that calling I said yes.

The details were worked out. I would assume pastoral duties immediately and would be there Sunday for both services that day. I would give a two week notice at work while the church would find a place for us to live. That Sunday we would work out the final details on moving arrangements and have lunch at the chairman of the deacon board's home.

There would be dinner at all the deacons' homes. Dinner at the song leader's home, dinner at the Sunday school teacher's home, dinner at most of the member's homes. The week's activities were already being planned, and the church people extended their Southern hospitality in every manner. I shall always remember the pride and excitement that these fine Christians showed in their pastoral decision process. They were feeling their way through this process, and they felt with their hearts. You could see it on their faces, and you could hear it in their voices. They were grateful to God that He had provided a pastor. I felt so terribly unworthy, greatly unqualified, and uniquely ready for this. There were no greater truths.

Chapter IX

"The Parting of the Red Sea"

The orange-and-white U-haul truck was already becoming too familiar to me. I knew the square footage and the amount of furniture these things could hold. I knew how to pack it, but I wasn't sure what was worthy to make the journey. My furniture was mostly secondhand and what was new was not top of the line. This was an aspect of the ministry I had never really thought about or expected to be so troubling. People would know everything about you. They would know your clothes, your finances, your life. They would know everything, and one assuming this role as pastor had to come to terms with it. You were a public figure, a celebrity of sorts and people liked to know everything about them. I had long ceased worrying about what people had thought about me, but this was altogether different.

All of a sudden I found myself caring very deeply about what people thought. It was now a matter of representing an office of the church. I was to be what they thought a man of God should be, have what a man of God should have, do what a man of God should do. But there was one sure thing that a man of God should not have; roaches.

Roaches were like the plague that never went completely away. For more than one hundred years this had been a Southern mill town. This meant a lot of people coming and going and a lot of leaving behind. Everyone had these creatures that they seemed to get rid of but would always came back. It was the poor man's curse. We had done everything we knew to do, and while we were finally rid of these pesky insects, we were always fearful because they would reappear at the worst of times. Times that were inconvenient and embarrassing. No suitable solution ever dismissed their presence or gave an accurate account of the chemical and biological warfare that had been waged to subdue these pests. They just seemed to appear when a nightlight was turned on. Everyone would express shock, like they had been beamed down by an alien space craft. The cockroach has survived everything Mother Nature has thrown at it short of the Apocalypse. So it was with guarded optimism we believed we could leave these creatures behind forever. I suppose there were a lot of things I wanted to leave behind; act as if they never happened, explain them away. However, with some things that was impossible. Even if the thing has the word *holy* attached to it.

When I was licensed to preach and then ordained, no one ever asked me if I had been married before. I had come from a respectable church whose pastor had been a member for many years. His pastoral leadership had been one of strict biblical doctrine as viewed by the denomination. So when the church and the pastor presented me for licensure and then latter ordination, it never crossed anyone's mind to ask the question, "Have you been married before?" It was not a marriage, but in the truthful light of day, vows were exchanged and God and everybody saw it. Yes, I had been married before. I had read Timothy and heard sermons on marriage, but I always figured it meant one wife at a time, not the husband of one woman. What in the world did that have to do with anything? It had a lot to do with everything. I just didn't know it until a Wednesday night service at my home church.

No one had arrived yet for the church service, and the pastor was seated in his office speaking with a man when I arrived. They spoke for a few minutes, and then the man left without any introductions or anything. He looked troubled, and while I was curious, I did not ask the pastor about the man's trouble. Instead he offered it in a mournful groan and said, "Poor fella, he loves the Lord so much and is doing his best for Him. But he has two living wives, and it's been real hard on him." I replied, "Better than two dead wives on your hand. That would be hard to explain." And I laughed. "No," he replied. "Not when you're trying to be a preacher. It's all but impossible." I cannot tell you the coldness that struck through my heart. It was like the police screaming, "Freeze!" It was like I had been caught stealing something, or the cashier lady was holding up my green free lunch card for all to see and yelling, "He's over here. What we gone do?" Indeed, what we gone do now?

I had come to the service to share the news of my acceptance of the pastoral duties I had tried out for. Now it seemed there was a great deal more to share than I had ever imagined. There was still time to undo what had been done and decline pastoral duties. I could continue working at the fire department. I had not left and no one had replaced my position. It was all a misunderstanding that was going to be taken care of. Everyone would want to do the right thing. There was no question about that. So I told him that I had been married before. After some probing questions concerning the woman and her location, her family, and the probability of encountering her regularly, he went somewhere for a few minutes. I don't know how long it was, but it seemed like a very long time. He returned, and the term annulment was mentioned.

The term described what I had been through because it was not a real marriage. It had been conceived in the insanity of my youth, born of a lie, my lie, and now it seemed it would die silently unopposed by any type of council. I had been married before, and it was that simple. The term annulment is a clean word for the sorrow and disappointment I put that young lady through. The burning issue of the hour was, Now what are we going to do? I remember asking the pastor how God could do such a thing. If this issue was of such great importance, why had God not addressed it before? Why was it not addressed by the pastor of the church I had joined? Why was the question of marriage not asked by the council that licensed me to preach and why not later by the ordaining council? If it was so life-and-death important, why had God called me to the ministry when it was contrary to the denomination's belief? I did not understand at all.

Being an older man with many years of experience as a pastor, he seemed to hear more in my questions than I realized when I had uttered them. Maybe he saw me walking away from God and His calling completely. Maybe the Holy Spirit so moved him, he could do only what he did. I cannot say the reason or motive. I believed he would do only what he knew and what he believed was right in the sight of God. Much later in life, after changing denominations to the Southern Baptist, I would be ordained in that denomination as a minister; a minister that had been married more than once. But this Wednesday evening, this question had to be settled, clearly settled. This pastor was a remarkable servant of God as I look back now. Contrary to what others may have thought or defined differently, he followed what he believed was the will of God. He so impressed upon my heart that a man will give an account of all that he is, but all that he was, had been forgiven and forgotten by God. He assured me all would be well and to go on about the Lord's business. I've often thought about that time he and I sat there, and I wondered what would have happened if things were done differently. Yet looking back, my clearest memory is the engrafted humility this experience left on my heart even today. Those who doubt God's ability to accomplish anything He chooses with anyone He chooses must not believe the story of Moses, David, and Paul. These men were guilty of murder, adultery, and genocide yet they accomplished their purpose for God. I did not know if I could accomplish what God was asking. I knew I was willing to pay any price, go any distance, and take any measure to try. Regardless of what others may think or believe it was time to get this show on the road.

This road would become so familiar to us. There would be many such roads in the years ahead. But no road is as important as the one you're on at the present time. I was not worried about what lay ahead down the road. I was just worried about making the trip that day. There was no great master plan, no route mapped out in this journey. It was simply the going. We'll find out when we get there. I miss that so much today. Shackled by schedules, money, or someone else's plans places unmovable detours which hinder such journeys of faith. A farmer once said to me, "Well, when you've never had anything to lose you don't know what it is to lose something." He had to sell a large piece of his property. I guess he was right in a way. This whole preaching business was in a sense like that. I didn't have anything to lose, or at least I thought I didn't.

The ordeal of arriving at a church with every worldly good you have displayed on the unloading ramp of a moving truck is borderline vulgar. The moment your furniture is unloaded your privacy ends, and your daily activities become posted through every form of communication known to man. Churches know what you're doing sometimes better than you do. It's hard for me to understand, but somehow protecting your privacy is very dangerous. The fact that your choices are guarded by reasons not spoken, or diminish in importance because of something else, is fertile ground for a lie. A wink or a nod or a plan never meant to be followed through. This solace of privacy is dangerous and affords far too many temptations. Satan even dared to tempt the Lord Jesus when He was by Himself in the desert.. Christian fellowship doesn't mean one is on display 24/7, but for the minister I'm afraid it does. Nothing catches the attention and imagination of church folk like the comings and goings of the preacher. Unless it is a drawer falling out of a chest with a pair of silk leopard-skin thong underwear floating down from the unloading ramp for God and everybody to see.

The sound of that drawer hitting that hard red clay caught everyone's attention. No one wanted to drop something or scratch anything. So the sound of something crashing compelled everyone to turn and see what had fallen. There floating in the air like a blimp over a sporting event was this pair of very sheer women's underwear. It was a moment in time in which heroes are born and true valor cannot be denied. No one could deny the heroics several elderly ladies displayed as they each took swipes at the passing garment. The underwear floated through their grasp like a dove through a peanut field full of spraying bird shot. The red-haired Sunday school teacher rocked back and forth on his heels as if he could not make up his mind if it was proper or not for him to be grabbing at ladies' underwear in front of everyone. His ruddy complexion seemed to get darker with every forward rock. Then with the speed of a striking rattler, his hand grabbed the underwear. There he stood, red-faced, grinning, and holding the silk leopard-skin underwear. His pride could not be contained. His expression was as if he had just pulled a drowning child from muddy waters. It's funny how brief moments of valor truly are. He had barely caught his breath before one of the women had snatched the underwear from his hand and tucked it back under the other clothing and replaced the drawer in the chest.

The roaches had vanished and never would be seen again, neither would the leopard-skin thong underwear. The entire experience went very well and the people could not have been more kind. They helped unpack, clean, and prepare a very nice meal for everyone. I could not imagine how God had pulled this off, but there I was. There was no turning back. The Red Sea had been parted, and there seemed to be no possible way to go back now, not even if someone wanted to.

Chapter X

"The Ten Commandments"

There are many rules in life. Some are pretty serious. Some are not very serious. The problem with rules is that they are made to be broken. Rules are written by men for men. Commandments come from God. There is no wiggle room on this one. It's a bottom line thing. We should take God's commandments very seriously. We should take with a grain of salt, however, some of the rules man has made in God's name. Knowing which is which is pretty simple. If God or His Son Christ Jesus says "This is a commandment I give you," well, there you go. There is no debate on this subject. Jesus said, "All authority in heaven and earth has been given unto me." You might think a new pastor has all the authority he needs to begin setting things in order. Nothing could be further from the truth. An older minister once said to me, "You can change this and change that but the next thing you'll be changing is your mailing address." No truer words were ever spoken to me.

Posted in the parsonage there should be the ten commandments that the church expects of the new pastor. Things he should do and things he should not do. Many problems would never occur if there was a clear understanding of what the minister should not even think about changing. The deacon board usually covers policy and procedure of church government and church plant operations.

The deacon board never addresses customs and rituals of colloquial worship. "Well that's the way we've always done that." "It was good enough for Papa Wilson. It's good enough for us." "It's just the way we do things around here." All these could be echoed a million times throughout the history of the church. Rural and city folk alike all sharing traditions passed on from one Daddy Rab to another. Unspoken rules instituted and forever ingrained in the spiritual character of the church.

At one church a woman prepared the bread for the Communion service. She had been taught in the preparation of the bread, but she had also been taught to bury the bread not used. So following every Communion service at dusk she would find herself a place in the woods near the graveyard and bury the remaining bread. Her husband's grandmother had done this during her lifetime, and the custom was passed down. That's the way of things in every church, in every land, and among every people. Some are just a bit stranger than others. I could have demanded that this practice be stopped and shown in church doctrine the error of such practice. I could have requested fellow ministers to come at a set time and address the performance of ordinances of the church. I could have. I could have done a number of things that were biblically correct and doctrinally sound, but choosing which one to do requires experience and common sense.

Since I had very little or no experience in matters such as this, I was inclined to trust prayer and common sense. Common sense will only get you so far because common sense can be slim pickings when it comes to changing things around a church. The issue of the Communion bread was privately discussed with the woman. Scriptures and common practice of sister churches were shared and that was that. Did I ask her if she complied? No. Did I launch a committee to observe her future practices? No. It really does not matter what I or anyone else believes or does not believe when it comes to making a change. If a change is needed you must present the need. Explain and justify the need and offer a correct alternative. The old saying, "You can lead a horse to water but you can't make him drink" is never more true. I've often wondered if that practice was passed on down to the next generation or not. I had done what I could do and what I believe the Lord would have me do. He had not sent me there to settle this issue once and for all. There were two other choices that I thought about. I could have eaten all the bread at the conclusion of the Lord's Supper, but that might have been a bit over the top. Or I could have requested someone else that believed like I did handle the preparation of Communion. That would have destroyed the unity of the church and made the spirit of Communion something it was not supposed to be. It was given by the Lord to gather His believers in remembrance of His sacrifice for the remission of the sins of the world. Communion is a gathering time not a dividing time. So in the changing of things around a church one must consider what is to be gained, what may be lost, and what price the church is willing to pay for this particular change. Because if you change some things somebody is going to pay for it in more ways than one.

Things had been going along very well. Church attendance was better than it had been in a long time. People seemed happy and believed they had made the right choice for a pastor. Church membership was progressing, and the offerings had improved along with the attendance. In general the church was attracting many young families. Keeping them was the challenge though. The average church member age was sixty years old, and the church building was over 160 years old. The church building sat on the original foundation, and remodeling of the building was last done ten years ago. The church needed a face-lift, arm-lift, and a lift in the seat of the britches to get off its bottom and get something done. I thought that was a good place to start; padded church pews, yes sir. That's what this church needed. Nothing like giving church members a more comfortable place to sit down to get them on their feet for

Jesus. Young preachers; we're so full of ourselves and our zeal for the Lord far outreaches the distance of our spiritual vision.

A company was contacted and the contract presented at a called business meeting. The church leaders filed in and sat in their pews. Every person has a seat in church, and for whatever reason they have chosen that seat. It is their seat. Of course they would surrender it for a guest at special services or visitors that didn't know better, but anyone in the church knows that they have always sat there. The fact that you could, from time to time, from church to church, see people's place change was a really good indicator that something was afoot. Where one sat in church was and will forever remain a mystery in the annals of how the Lord moves in mysterious ways. People on the other hand are very demonstrative in assuming their seat position. Sunday school books, handbags, blankets, sweaters, why I have even seen Bibles left in pews to mark the territorial borders. It reminded me of Christmas Eve at our house growing up as children. Each child left their shoes in front of the place Santa was to leave their Christmas presents. Same thing here. I guess people felt a small portion of ownership, and I think it was a good thing. I believe everyone should have their place in God's house. A place of comfort that gives them a sense of belonging, a place that is so familiar to them it offers security and a moment of rest. I just could not believe the lengths that people were willing to go to protect that hallowed ground.

The matter was discussed and I had a moment. It was these moments in pastoral planning that you find yourself writing about thirty years after the fact. My idea was to have this project of padding the pews funded by each family donating the money for that particular pew. The church would place a small bronze plate on the end of the pew with the name of someone the pew was dedicated to; a family member or someone who had been a member of the church and had now passed away. Oh, I thought it was a grand idea and so did everyone present. The motion was passed, received a second, and so shall it be, oh me.

The various families were called or handed in cards with the name of a departed family member. Each name brought with it the story of that person's church history and how they singlehandedly had kept the church from going under. Most names were the names of mothers or fathers. Each name was proudly presented, and while some of the names were familiar some were not. Extensive research was done insuring proper spelling of the departed church members' names. That meant looking in the back of old family Bibles and then being able to decipher the penmanship. The bronze plates were engraved as directed by the donor family and the pew where they were to be placed was chosen. Well, some thought they were chosen. When two or three donor families began choosing the same pew, disgruntled donors rose up. After much discussion among themselves, the matter was settled by date of death. The last deceased church member would receive first place and so forth. That issue was settled. The pews were padded, plates placed on pews, but now families were standing in the isles refusing to sit anywhere else except where they had placed that bronze plate. They had laid claim to this pew. Money had changed hands.

A retired cook in the navy was a church member and stayed on the telephone all the time. He was a talker. I never heard of a problem or a possible conflict in which his name was not somehow involved. Sometimes it was him calling and giving a shot across the bow, or just checking to see how rough the seas would be. He loved navy talk. He loved the Navaho tribe talk. He loved the Zulu talk. This man loved to talk, and talk, and talk. It was his unrestrained zeal for the English language, however, which seemed to always get him in the middle of everything. He loved being in the middle of it whatever it was. He had two cents and he spent it like it was a dollar. He also had a deceased family member in the church, and he had purchased a bronze engraved plate in memory of his dear departed loved one. A Sunday morning had come and the pews were padded and the bronze engraved plates adorned the end of each pew. It was a beautiful morning, and the people seemed very proud that the church looked nice.

The cook walked down the center aisle of the church with his wife and stopped at the pew he had placed a memorial plate on. Another member of the church was sitting there. It was the same member he had been talking to and about all week But it was high noon now. Apparently there had been dares and double dares going on all week, and it was coming to a show down. A showdown right in front of the new preacher, God, and everybody else. The cook favored Rodney Dangerfield. He had these huge bulging eyes, and his face could turn red as a beet in about a nanosecond. When he got excited, his voice squealed and screeched as every word added volume and tempo to his delivery. It was like Don Knotts on steroids. The cook's wife was a character in her own right, but she was a lovely lady, kind and considerate with a huge generous heart. Her brother was a pastor, and maybe because of that she was more keenly aware of other people's feelings. However, she was a navy wife and that meant, right or wrong ,she was to stand her man. The tension was trembling the Sunday morning bulletin the cook held in his hand. His eyes were closed, and like a racing fire the redness rushed from his neck to the top of his head. It was like the animation in a Saturday morning cartoon. I kept expecting his head to explode or start spinning around and around. His eyes were bugling out of their sockets, and I rehearsed the initial assessments of cardiopulmonary arrest. I don't know what happened next. I looked down at the floor for a minute, and sensed that everyone in the church was looking at me to see what I was going to do. Perhaps like Moses I would stand, raise a wooden staff, and part waters or something. I knew it was a sentinel event in pastoral authority. These church members knew exactly what was happening. They wanted to see what I would do. I know what I wanted to do, but I had no idea what to do.

It is amazing the number of times human beings are faced with the critical reckoning of an event of which they have no idea what should be done. I've seen young paramedics run around in circles as bodies lay smoldering in a house fire. I've seen parents so overcome by disbelief in what their eyes were showing them that they were blinded to the reality that their child was dead. The flight or fight sympathetic switch is not bumped. You know something must be done, you just don't know what to do. I must have had a deer-in-the-headlight look, and that was a look I did not want the church to see. It was their right to expect leadership from God's man. So with that thought in mind I looked toward the song leader, gave him a nod, and the service began. The man and his wife walked out of the church with no escalation of the drama. They would return in a small measure of time when there was something else to talk about. It would not take too long for that to come about.

Homecoming was an annual event which any church worth its salt always addressed with most serious measure. The food issue was settled many years ago, and this year would be no different. The flavors of the food would be like a vapor in the humid Southern air. There was no former pastor alive so I would be speaking that morning. The attendance would triple for this service as many would travel from many places to attend. Parents brought children back. Children brought parents back. The grounds were mowed and hedges trimmed. Flowers were placed on every table. Seats were set up outside for those who could not find a seat inside. It was a pretty big deal and resembled a scene out of a movie. It was a darling picture of believers. Darling smiles. Darling embraces and no grander chance to catch up on local news and the latest gossip. That was fine with me. After all, we are just people, and people are human with weak and frail imperfections. We live and are sustained by God's grace alone. He does things for us when we have no idea that He has done them. There is no possible avenue accessible to the mind of man to comprehend all that God does, has done, and will do. Man's conscious efforts to comprehend and repay God for such loving care are bewildering. Being totally bewildered would also describe my efforts to merit this most gracious time in my life.

I did consider it a most gracious time. I knew that even then. The very moment I had arrived at the church I realized within my heart how wonderful it was to be a pastor. It was not the authority, the position, or the responsibility. It was this love which burned in my heart for God. It was this incredible time in my life which God for some reason had allowed me to be at this church. I suppose I did what I did during this time of homecoming to attempt to protect this precious gift. I suppose I did what I did thinking that I was keeping the ministry focused on the purpose of God. I thought everyone would see the merit in my pastoral decision and my desire to keep this homecoming free of anything that would distract from these darling of days.

The church membership consisted of several people that held elected offices in the county. The county tax officer, members of the board of education, the sheriff ,and many others who sat on some form of board or other were members of the church. The political season was afoot, and many were up for election. The county was known statewide for it's political activity. Characters were plentiful in the days preceding the election. Rumors and counter-rumors came and went. For the most part, these were Americans in their finest hour. They were good people and good citizens who really believed in their choices. They knew that the only way to really know the truth about what was going on in local government was to run for local government. They had seen questionable things done in past administrations when contracts or laws were passed seemingly favoring one family or part of the county. Nothing stood the political hair on end on the back of their necks as when these facts appeared in the local newspaper. Investigators took on operations the CIA would envy. Spies crawled through the court house, and undercover operations were designed to trap or uncover any mischief. Not that there was any going on, but it was the season. The longevity of office depended more on the ability to quell any misinformation and correctly identify its source. This process, however, could possibly involve the DA's office but more than likely it was a matter of DNA.

Families, friends, and neighbors chose their political horse and hung on for the ride because it was not only a ride it was a race. A race that was exciting and full of unexpected events that could determine many aspects of people's lives for several years to come. For this reason, I wanted the church to be neutral territory where all people could come and worship the Lord. I had heard war stories about past elections with characters right out of Southern novels. I wanted none of that for the church so I did what I thought was right. I suppose I did what I did believing that somehow I was keeping the church out of controversy, out of harm's way, not realizing that it was the church that would be in the center of everything. The church members were the candidates. The church membership was the friends or family of the candidates. The church membership had three men who were running for the office of sheriff. There was no way the church was not going to be in it.

In the movie *Walking Tall*, a man was elected by the people to take back the countryside from the lawless heathen. While hardly any county can boast of such legendary characters in today's law enforcement, these sheriff candidates were trying to establish their own character. The three men in church running as candidates were as different as day and night. Two were honest and decent men and their families had been in that area for many generations. These two men attended church and maintained their Christian testimony throughout the entire election. This was not to say that there were not a few rifts along the way, but most of these were a result of overzealous friends or family. These two men were the kind of men that you would be proud to call your friends. They were good men and attended church regularly. The third man, however, was a man with a lot of church history but no real presence.

This man's family had been in this county for many generations. In fact, his father had been sheriff for about twenty-five years in this county. I never met his father as he had died a year or two before my arrival. I had never met this man who was running for sheriff. I knew his name, the history of his family, and the legend of his father who they called "Bull." Stories abounded, whether true or not, about how Bull used to drag black men behind his sheriff's car, how he took prisoners, black and white, into the swamp and they never came out. Rumors about drugs and moonshine flowed through the county like the ripples on a spring creek. It seemed everything that I heard painted a picture of a smart old man who was sheriff for twenty-five plus years. That does not happen being careless or stupid. The struggle for his office was documented in papers all across the South. Since I was not there, it would be neither here nor there for me to attempt to validate or dispute any one's recollection of an event during Bull's life. I could validate, however, that our homecoming Sunday rested in the latter part of the election season, and political tensions were higher than they had been in quite some time. With that in mind, I made the pastoral decision to lessen political influence of the day and focus on godly worship by asking the church to honor a pastoral request:. If you were a member of the church and running for public office that year, you must abstain from singing, tap-dancing, or anything at homecoming service so as to remove any appearance of politics. I wanted the service to remain a time of worship and not to give the Devil a chance to muddy the water. Well, everybody thought it was a good idea.

It was two days before homecoming when the telephone rang, and it was the navy cook ready to stir the pot. Had I been in a smarter frame of mind I would have hung the phone up, but this was long before caller ID and call waiting or he would have been waiting until Jesus came. I knew the sound of his voice. I knew before he said a word that the words which would come from his mouth, no matter what they were, would sound the general quarters call for all hands on deck and to man the battle stations. I could smell the gunpowder as he began, "Preeeeeacherrrrr. You remember the rule you made bout homecoming, and that noooobody was to sing and stuff, well … one man is bringing his band with him, and they are planning to sing all afternoon. Just thought you needed to know. You know he's running for sheriff, preacher." Right then was when somebody should have taken a hammer and a sixteen-penny nail and nailed a stupid sign right in the center of my forehead. A bright orange sign with red writing saying, "Here is a stupid preacher about to prove how stupid a preacher can be if you give him the chance." I was so angry.

I was angry at the man who called me and at the man who planned to sing. I was angry at God who had sent me to this place. But the truth of the matter was, I was simply angry. Anger and stupidity are forever joined together and just kind of pull each other around like hitched wagons. If you could take the time and think about stupidity, you would not get angry. If you really thought about anger you would really see how stupid anger is, but the truth is you can't see but one thing at a time even though they are joined at the hip. Stupidity and anger are so volatile because one usually appears by itsself, but the other is soon to follow.

I hung the phone up and mulled the thing over in my mind for several minutes. I considered the source of the information, but realized that by now the entire county was being made aware that the Reverend had been notified. Now everyone would see if this young preacher means what he says and says what he means. I'm sure he had added a good deal of colorful commentaries suggesting that he had an insider's knowledge of my intent and reason. I believe his nephews or nieces who grew up around him might have gone to work at Fox news or CNN. Talking heads exist to talk about something, whether they know anything about it or not. Talk, talk, and talk about other people who are talking and about others who are not talking. The gentleman who was among the others running for sheriff and was the one who planned to sing owned and operated a used car lot. That should tell you something. I know it did me. But

I laid aside all of my personal experiences of men that had sold me cars that cost too much, ran too little, or offered deals of a lifetime. Nothing could be more true, however, than the deal he was about to offer me. It would be a once-in-a-lifetime experience.

He answered the phone at the car lot. When I told him who I was, and that I would like to talk to him when he had the time to do so he replied, "I'll be right there." He wasn't lying. I had poured myself a fresh cup of coffee and had added the creamer, but before the color had changed from black to a golden brown he was knocking on the front door. I had not even told him where I lived or anything, but there he stood. He was standing like he came out of a picture made in the fifties. His black hair was as black as his teeth were white. The sun's rays reflecting off that greased-down black hair made me squint. His face was wet and shiny too, and his brilliant blues eyes revealed the excitement of his hurried response. Looking back now I realize he thought he was about to receive an endorsement for the office of high sheriff. I guess, but to tell you the truth I don't know what he was thinking. But there he stood all right, with one hand in his pocket and the other outstretched for some serious handshaking.

We sat down in the living room, and I slowly began to explain what I had said about the homecoming service. If any member was running for any county office, they were to restrain themselves on this special day from any appearance of campaigning. This was a historical day for the church and represented a lot of sacrifices that many families had made over the years to keep the church doors open. I said everything that I could think of that would make his agreement sound as if he was a willing martyr. His agreement would be a challenge for all the faithful to see that his recognition of that day deserved everyone's acknowledgement of God's special blessings on this church. He replied, "No preacher I won't be there, no sir." And he wasn't or at least not in person.

The morning was everything it was supposed to be. It was indeed a sight to see; all those white tablecloths spread on those concert tables. The women's choice of dresses varied in every manner but particularly in color. There were so many colors the congregation looked like a spring flower garden. Most of the faces were of people I did not recognize. They had traveled here that morning to bring Mother back for possibly her last homecoming service at her old church. Emotions were as plentiful as the bouquet of color. At some point in the service, the youngest member, the oldest member, or other special person would be recognized for some honor or past contribution. Careful planning went into this. The last thing you wanted was a crying jag right in the middle of the festivities. None of that happened. It was going to be a picture perfect day. Everything was wonderful. Every available seat was taken by cheerful, smiling people as they waved to others sitting across the church. Children had pleasant expressions as they too expected something wonderful to begin at any moment, and so it did.

Miss Inez came running down the center aisle of the church in full gallop. The soles of her shoes were clicking and clapping like that of running horses. The sound echoed throughout the sanctuary. The expression on her face and drawn lips assured me Jesus had come, and we were getting up a bus load right then and there. I wish that had been true. Oh, how I wished I could have looked up and seen the sweet Savior's face. I wish I could have seen Saint Peter, heard the angel Gabriel blowing on that golden trumpet, and seen all the angels filling the skies, heaven bound. But all that filled my sight was a black man in a purple tux, pink shirt, and yellow polka-dot tie, carrying the biggest Bible I've ever seen in my life.

Miss Inez's narrative accompanied the scene like a professional sports forecaster. My eyes followed her description like a running brook trails down a stream, every little turn cascading downstream filling in any possible void. She described it perfectly.

She began, "Preeeaccchhherrr, there's black man with a Bible under his arrrrrm, and he's a-comin' in the church." Her eyes were fixed on me like she expected me to start shouting orders as if we were under fire during a surprise attack in the middle of the siege of Atlanta. Her teeth were clenched and you could actually hear them grinding under the tremendous strain her GI tract was under. I feared blindness was nearing for her. Nevertheless, like a brave soldier of the cross she stood there, white purse strung across one arm, the other cradling the Word of God awaiting any orders from command. I said, "Thank you Miss Inez and good morning." She went blank. No expression. I could not discern any visible effort to breathe. I've never seen anyone go that long without blinking her eyes. Then she slowly turned toward her seat, and upon seeing the man sitting down on the front row between two elderly white women I heard a faint gasp. She walked toward her pew hunched over as if she was ready for a fifty-yard sprint if the man so much as looked toward her. She could have run it too. She was eighty-plus years but as solid as the oaks in her front yard. She sat down, and I could see the congregation was paying more attention to her than the black man. The South was changing and had changed a great deal but the most segregated time in the South is Sunday morning between eleven and noon.

Even today, thirty-some years later, it remains mostly true. The truth simply is that there is a vast difference between the method, style, and preference in worshiping God. Blacks have a more demonstrative expression of worship in some of their churches while in some white churches you need to take a pulse to see if anyone is alive. Most black and white churches lie somewhere in the middle of these characteristics, and many still prefer their private time with God. Aside from these characteristics, most churches in the South are family churches. One or two or three families have kept the church going for many years and find it distressing allowing too many outsiders considering the business of the church. It's a control thing. When things were under control, there was less to worry about, and one could concentrate on the sin business. The sin business had been and would long be big business in the churches of the South. It was unfortunate, however, that the focus was on somebody else's sin and not one's own. Lord help us all. The Lord truly helped me that morning.

Sermon selection for homecoming or any special occasion is pretty simple really. Of course you pray about it, but you really embrace the meaning of the occasion and use biblical principles to reinforce current goals that the church may have at the present time. You always mention the history of the church and deceased members who contributed to the well-being of the church. If you mention visiting relatives from out of town who are visiting the church that day, well, now you have got a winner that they'll talk about over the fried chicken. Nothing quite moves the heart of a preacher more than to hear these words slide across a pair of greasy lips, "That was a mighty fine sermon there dis morning, preacher." One could only prepare and give one's best effort, trusting God for the results regardless of the chosen text or subject. That morning text and subject were not a homecoming message, and I had no idea why I was preparing to deliver a sermon on homosexuality, but God did.

Homosexuality, even though it began with the same letter as homecoming, was about as far from the meaning of the day's occasion as anything. It ruled out all the possibilities of mentioning former members and being able to remain in the same county. It sure did not embrace any current drives to stamp out or embrace homosexuality. It was a sin sermon. Homosexuality is a sin problem. It is no different than any other sin that will send an unrepentant heart to an everlasting godless torment. Sin. Sin. Sin. It's like Deputy Barney Fife told his pastor after sleeping through the morning's sermon, "You can never hear enough about sin." These kinds of sermons rarely trouble the church because for the most part it is not guilty of homosexual practices. They can say "amen" all day and never say "oh me" once! It was a fire and brimstone sermon, and I kind of hit all the top ten sins of the day. Nothing quite whets the appetite for a meal than burning calories contributing a few "amens" to the pastor's effort. As Mama Rab would say, "A good time was had by all." The black man came and went without anyone saying anything or even paying a great deal of attention, but apparently it caught God's attention.

Four or five days later the phone rang and the deep baritone voice speaking on the other end of the phone identified himself as apostle Leftston. He said, "Reverend, that man that came to your church last Sunday was not a member here at our church. In fact I put him out of the church because he has gay spirit on him. Therefore when it was proven to the church, I had no choice but to put him out of the church. The fact that the man drove from your church, Reverend, to a man's house running for sheriff ought to tell you something." It did. The very man I had asked not to sing in a gospel group and abide by my pastoral decision against campaigning had paid this man to dress up in that purple tuxedo, pink shirt, and yellow bow tie. I'm sure that the fact that he happened to be the only known black homosexual in the county had nothing to do with him being selected as well.

All I was trying to do was prevent an opportunity for Satan to cause trouble at a time when the church did not need any. But instead it was turned into a day I will never forget as long as I live. I was still learning.

I was writing my sermons and using colored highlighters for prompting tempo and point expression. It was working very well. I tried to find an hour or so during the week to practice the delivery and had figured out how many sheets of notes it would require for a thirty or forty minute sermon. Regardless, I knew that at noon I had to have the Lord's business taken care of. Nothing lessens the effect of a good sermon than watchful eyes on the clock. People have their Sundays planned, and for many it is not a restful day. They had to get up for Sunday school, the morning worship service, and then the evening service. This meant I had taken three or four hours of their day already. Then figure in the time for a meal, a football game, a nap, and a hurried ride back to church. That left many faithful weary, but they still came. They came and kept coming. Their faces were becoming very familiar, and I now put names of wives, husbands, and children together in the proper family. This was and still is no small task for any preacher, but some men have mastered a method of word association to recall names and faces. I never was that scientific about the process. I simply asked everyone to tell their name every so often, and it would help me to learn not only their names but things about them. Repetitive introductions always brought with them new information about their lives and the news in their families. I stood at the back door every Sunday morning and waited for them to pass, and if I was able to call their names as they approached, I would always see smiles on their faces. I visited every home that I could as often as I could but nothing strikes fear in the heart of a parishioner more than the preacher standing at the door. The home's appearance and odors told more about the people that lived in them than their speech. Cigarette smoke, brewing coffee, magazines, and the sounds of whatever was playing on the radio or television were clearly there for all to see. But as these people came down the aisle toward the door leaving the church, they were at their Sunday best.

There is an art to standing at the doorway of a church and speaking to a congregation. Each conversation has to be authentic and personal while expressing proper responses to a sundry of parting adieus. Polite phrases such as "Thank you" and "Have a good day" forwarded to those who passed at a quicker pace seemed well, but this would be considered a slight if given to a person who desired a moment of conversation. This could only be determined by reading the face, the posture, and the pace of one's gait as he or she passed. The pastoral duties for the day were not over until every soul had left and you were locking the doors. Even as you did this you recounted the sermon, the conversations, the prayers offered during the day, and the parting comments because some would remain with you through time.

The months came and went. I was learning more and more about being a pastor and about people. This was a gift of God. This group of people, while not great in number, was as vastly different as they could be. I learned different things from different encounters. I learned more from my first funeral about sorrow and grief than any heart of man could ponder. An awkward woman who was very poor attended church every once in awhile. Her house was literally falling down. The front porch was slanted almost forty-five degrees, and you had to lean forward to traverse to the front door. Her teeth were horrible. The clothes she wore must have been selected at Goodwill when times were better for she had had them for a while. But she did have a phone, and she did call me about preaching a funeral for her niece who had a child pass away. I was surprised to hear that it was a little three-year-old girl. This niece had gotten pregnant by the boy who worked on a farm, and he had left her. She had lived with her father and mother in a sharecropper's home. The owner of Coca Cola had bought thousands of acres of land many years ago in the surrounding three counties and had a plantation of sorts. It was a vast vision of what the old South was in previous years. Long, winding clay roads and little white wooden houses were all built alike for the supervisors of the farm. This girl's father was the ramrod of the farming efforts. He managed several black families that lived in smaller houses and drove the tractors and equipment for the upkeep of this vast endeavor. He also trained the bird dogs for the quail hunts that men would fly in for from all over the world. Movie stars and famous sports athletes would fly in from time to time for hunts. The plantation still exists there today and so does the memory of my first funeral.

It was raining that early morning, and it was cold. The long clay road was muddy, and I was still driving the old 1972 Chevy

Nova with three speed on the column. The doorjambs had rubber inserts from the factory, but they had dry rotted and when it rained a little water might splash up on my trousers. This morning it was red muddy water splashing on the only real suit I owned. I could have driven for NASCAR the way I was shifting gears and slipping and sliding on that Georgia red clay. The hills required special effort because the shifter was subject to hang up in gear if done too quickly. I followed the directions as best I could, but I had driven ten miles or more down this red clay road and all I was seeing were fields of harvested peanuts and corn. The rain was easing up, but my left lower leg was soaking wet and my shoes were covered in red muddy water. As I was just about to stop and turn around I was met by three white pickup trucks. Each truck was full of black men waving for me to follow them. They all had on green overalls with the name of the plantation sewed on the right chest area. The driver of the lead truck appeared to be in charge of this procession. He chewed on a big cigar and drove with one arm hanging out of the window as if this swerving was as normal as driving in the parking lot at Wal-Mart. Then suddenly we slowed down, too slow, for in front of us the road had a creek crossing the roadway. Well, it looked like a creek anyway. The trucks had mud grips on their rear wheels, but my little blue Nova had slick worn tires on, and I knew I was going to get stuck in that running water. So I sped up coming up on the bumper of the truck ahead of me. We rocked and slid through it all right, but the water splashed up on the plug wires of the motor, and my car started spitting back and trying to cut off. Steam started coming out from under the hood and the dash. Every brake that I had on the car suddenly just vanished. It was on then. If the house had not been so close, I would have never made it to my first funeral, but I rolled up into the yard like Richard Petty at Daytona, smoke coming from everywhere.

I sat in the car trying to gain my composure. The windows were steamed up and the wipers were dragging across the windshield, thumping like a flat tire on every swipe. I turned everything off and gathered up my Bible making sure the paper clips marking selected Scripture and hidden notes had not been dislodged in the last heat race. I looked in the mirror of the car and there was even red mud on my face. God, are you there? I always believed, and still do believe that God is always with us, seeing about us, and taking care of us in times of need. I just wanted to ask Him how He liked the ride. But all that was forgotten when I could see through the windshield . Standing there under a small black tent with the words Remington Firearms printed on it stood the young girl, her clothes wet, her hair wet, her face wet, her heart wet from the tears of her soul spilling down her face. She was a sorrowful sight of woe. She trembled in the cold wind as her father stood beside her. He was a giant of man. Nearly six foot seven, he too had on green overalls and boots that looked like they just came out of the fields. His face was dark colored and his hands were white and ashy and were attached to tree trunks that hung by his side. The black men got out of their trucks, walked, and stood behind the man in the rain. All the men were looking at this huge man, and in their eyes there was genuine concern. They stood and folded their hands as they held their hats. Everyone was looking at me sitting in that little blue Nova.

I got out of the car, lost in the scene that stood before me. On the casket platform rested a pink-and-white cardboard coffin. It was made of pressed paper which was used in pauper's coffins. At the sight of this small coffin sprinkled with raindrops, it seemed like the tears of God fell on this little casket. I was so moved and so emotional that I felt my eyes begin to water, and I took a deep breath knowing this was not about me. It was not about the ride, not about the mud, but about God's business. The first text Jesus ever preached in church was from Isaiah, chapter sixty-one. The sense of duty was so real I could hardly contain myself. Yet I had been an ambulance driver. I had seen scenes when men panicked and out of the sense of duty did more harm than good. I knew how to remain cool, calm, and collected. I heard Big Jim saying, "Don't worry about the mule, just load the wagon."

I don't remember the text and all that I said, but I remember it was acceptable and the family appreciated it. When I had completed the service, I stood in front of that girl who never looked me in the face. It was as if I was death itself summoning a final reckoning of what was next; the lowering of her little girl into a grave. For it was not me she refused to see, it was the rain that had filled the bottom of the vault into which her precious love would be lowered. I shook the father's callused hands and offered my final words of comfort. They stood around the coffin under that little tent. I did not know what to do, but they seemed to want to be alone so I turned to walk back to the car. The father called to me and then ran toward me with a wet envelope in his hand and gave it to me. "It ain't much, preacher, but it's all we got," he whispered. I got in the car and by God's grace it fired up, and I pulled down in low gear and eased out of the driveway. I stopped looking at the water still rushing across the roadway and took a moment trying to remember how I got across last time. When I looked in the mirror, I saw the girl faint into her father's arms. He carried her inside the home. I put the car in neutral and walked to the porch of the house where I was greeted by the father. "Is she okay?" I asked. "She'll be all right," he replied. "How about you, sir?" I asked. "I'll be all right," he said and turned and walked toward the tent as the men began to shovel the dirt on the grave. I wrote a song entitled "I'll Be All Right" many years later. I still play and sing it. I still cry when I remember my first funeral. On the outside of the envelope written in smeared pencil was the word *prachar*. Inside was $13.53. But what I took away from there, money could not buy or ever replace. God was there. I had given everything I had to give. I had tried to comfort this poor girl when her heart was torn into pieces. In the process it left enduring scars on my heart which always make me mindful of the scars Jesus bore because He cared about and loved us.

The phone would ring from time to time, and I'd be off on some kind of mission. Sometimes it would be sickness somewhere or a death. A death vigil might last for days, sitting in the family waiting room at some hospital for a few hours with the family as the dying business took place. Families were weird sometimes about what they did and what they believed to be important at times like this. People needed the pastor to come and get the latest news of the family member's status which took precedence over all pastoral duties.. I knew the prognosis on many such occasions and knew these statements of faith were simply the desires of the heart. I found that these moments were valuable moments in which a pastor could observe and listen to the conversations of the family. In these conversations different roles within the family were defined and a bereavement pecking order was established. If any violations occurred as to who would be the next to go in the intensive care unit, they were quietly handled in the inflexible Southern folkways.

These folkways were often no more than a nod or the patting of a chair for the person to have a seat and think about his or her request. There were those that wailed and slept on the floor or some walked around the hospital grounds outside in small groups. The young were never excluded and were allowed more flexible behaviors depending on the situation. There would be stepfathers, in-laws, and outlaws. Long-standing family feuds and personal prejudices had to be addressed in a sensitive manner. If the pastor was smart, he avoided these issues and never committed to assisting in any final decision about anything. When pressed or drawn into reaching a final resolution concerning what was the proper thing to do, the pastor would be wise to refer to the words of Jesus, "Judge not lest thou also be judged." It worked most of the time, but there were these moments when civility cried out for an immediate remedy. Such was the case in my own family.

The phone rang in the middle of the night. Never a good sign. It was a veterans' hospital in Florida where my father was a patient.

The physician told me he was to have an emergency operation in the morning. They were going to remove his left lower leg due to the dangerous possibility of blood clots traveling from there to his brain or heart that would kill him. I told the surgeon that I would be there the next morning. I did not sleep at all that night.

The night in slow motion presented the effects of his life on mine which ran across scenes burned in my memory of childhood. They were painful, sad, and pushed by a sense of undeniable loss. The loss of childhood, the loss of family and friends, the loss of having a father who was not there for moments when a child needs the counsel of a father. Satan never misses an opportunity to weary the mind and body of a Christian. He punches and jabs at the emotions that are raw nerves and sends our imaginations and human limitations of understanding beyond the vale of comprehension. The hours passed slowly, and there were moments when I yielded to anger, resentment, and the sense that once again he was robbing me of normalcy. Yet the early morning hours brought with them the sense that I was ready to lay aside all these silly ideas of self and go see about my father. I was ready.

A good pastor will always have a pressed white shirt and suit hanging ready in the closet for these midnight calls. You not only had to fulfill the role of pastor, but it was a customary expectation that you arrive dressed out for the game. I was taught by example rather than the letter of the law about these pastoral expectations. I dressed and again set out on a journey through the highways of south Georgia into Florida. I was born in Tallahassee and the hospital was several miles south. All this seemed new to me as I had not been back to Florida for many years. I arrived at the hospital in time to see my father before surgery. As I walked down those dim hallways to his room, my heart raced, and I searched for the proper words to say to this man. I had seen him briefly over the years when he would catch a bus and come during Christmas. His stay was always brief and always left me wanting to forget it. I suppose

I was coming to terms with all this history with every step. When I entered the doorway of his room, I knew I had arrived at the place where my daddy was.

The small overhead light was on, and he lay on his back looking out the window as the sun was breaking over the top of the sapling pines by the parking lot. The room smelled of Betadine and old clothes. As I looked at him, I saw a thin, pale man with this head full of black shiny hair. I wondered what he was thinking, if he had been told I was coming, or was he wondering if I'd really come at all. I could not help it. I could not contain myself. I didn't say anything, nor did he. I just simply bent down and hugged him for what seemed like hours. We both had tears in our eyes when the embrace was over. Words were not needed. Fathers and sons can do that. I recalled the story of the prodigal son Jesus had talked about and somewhere along the way it had become a physical part of who I am today. It was about forgiveness, forgiveness for both of us. I told him I loved him, and we spoke of the operation. He told me I did not have to stay for the whole operation, that he would be fine. I wish I could remember all that we spoke about but I cannot. It was just small talk, family stuff, but he never asked about my brothers or sister. I suppose they were each their own individual memory. I heard the stretcher's wheels wobbling down the hallway as they were coming to get him. We prayed together, and he was gone.

He made it through surgery, had been taken to the recovery room, and then back to his room. After surgery was completed, I spoke with the surgeon and told him I would return tomorrow because he told me my father was sleeping and needed rest. That night the phone rang again, but this time the news was not good. The hospital staff had found him dead in his bed in his room during the night. He had died alone in a veterans' hospital.

I remember calling Mother first to tell her that he had died. What I heard surprised me to no end. She was heartbroken. Her voice trembled and she wept. She sobbed. I guess in her heart she still saw him as a Korean War veteran coming home from a hellish war. She still had within her heart the memories of their better life, when they were young and their dreams were possible. During the fifties jobs were plentiful, and he had done well at a few of them but the bottle always won. It always destroyed, but he would always try again in the beginning. We called my brothers and sister and told them of Father's death. There were no tears. I cannot remember their emotions or words, but I remember the effort my mother offered to have all of her children attend their father's funeral. I was going to be there, of course. I had to preach his funeral.

It seems odd that as I reflect on my pastoral efforts for my own family. Emotions surfaced at unexplained times for undefined reasons. Seeing a family dealing with the beast of grief and uncertainty summons a glimpse of these moments even today. It allows me the privilege of offering a family direction from the memories of my own journey through these dark days of mourning and duty.

I sat beside my mother's bed at the Hospice House where she lay in the final days of her life. My brothers and sister had been active in staying with her through the process of the pancreatic cancer's prognosis. She had developed wet breathing sounds throughout both lung fields. Her breathing was rapid and shallow. I knew this woman, who had sacrificed everything for her children, had given all she could give. She refused offers to come to my house and any offers of help, and looking back I realize that she was weary of the struggle. The oncologist had given her twelve to forty days to live. This was the twelfth day. She had been in the hospital, but when the physicians offered no hope they advised us to place her in a hospice program. I wanted her to go home with me, but she refused. I believe the possibility of her depending on yet another household in providing her rest and refuge was unacceptable. This was the finish line of the race she had started years ago when we had ran for our lives in the darkness from our troubled home. The years and miles since then were salted with moments when she had to accept help along the way from family and friends. While they gave out love and she never doubted their motives, she had grown weary of the needing. She died a poor woman. She owned no home, no property, no place of her own to die. Her dignity was regal in those hours. I had told her the diagnosis and was honest about the prognosis, a fact that my sister found unacceptable. She became so angry at me for being honest with Mother that she left the hospital and never returned, not even to my mother's funeral. She had her own demons. The childhood we shared together had deposited something within all of us. Things uniquely grotesque and personally self-destructive walked in the shadows of our lives. Things sociologists and physiologists label deviant, or some other fifty-cent word to explain things they have only witnessed and never experienced. It is like trying to explain being wet when one has never felt the water. Things were there, however, moving in and out of our lives and leaving behind wounds inflicted on the moral conscience and compass. Some wounds were deadly.

At a church in Alabama, I received a call from my youngest brother. He was in trouble. He asked to stay with me for a few days. He arrived late one afternoon, and we went fishing. It was a beautiful evening, and a time when men share their deepest feelings. Maybe it's the water, the wildlife, or the peace of the water in the cool part of a summer's day. Whatever the tonic, it seems to sooth the worries of a busy or troubled mind. It was a listening time. A time of meditation when one's own soulful expression flows as freely as the water's current.

It was not easy to listen to his confession as we fished that beautiful evening. The summer's water temperature had the largemouth bass in shallow water, and we were fishing with top water plugs. The action was fast as the bass were striking our baits with almost every cast. I thought this was good and would take his mind off of his troubles if only for a moment. Then suddenly a huge bass hit his lure. He managed the battle properly, but the big fish came to the surface and started to shake his head back and forth trying to shake the lure loose from his mouth. Then suddenly the lure flashed in the air. The big fish rolled on his side from exhaustion and then slowly sank into the depths of the river. He had lost it. I shall never forget his words as we watched the bass disappear in the dark waters. "It's like everything else in my life. It's gone," he said. He cried and told me what had happened. That in itself left a pitiful distortion of reality within me. Somehow I saw him as the victim, but in truth he was only the victim of his own mind. The accompanying villain had been with him, with all of us, and we each unknowingly dealt with it as best we could. He was not successful.

I was teaching a series on the family on Wednesday nights at the church I was pastoring at that time. I told him about it and said if he wanted to go to church with us that would be great. The lesson was not for his benefit as the series had been going on for weeks. He declined the invitation and stayed home. Later that night while we were sleeping, he got up and took my son's shotgun and shot himself in the head. He had walked out of the driveway of the parsonage, took a few steps, and then pulled the trigger. Two weeks later I would find the darkened asphalt marker where he ended his life.

As I looked down at this place, I could see what I had seen many times before at shootings. This time it was different. This time there were violent screaming accusations of betrayal and failure. My betrayal, my failure to help him when he needed it the most. Failure to recognize all the classic signs of premeditated suicide. Failure and betrayals known only by me and the Wicked One for it was he that was screaming in my thoughts.

The apostle Paul wrote about the spiritual warfare Christians encounter as he pled for them to realize that in this world the Evil One is very powerful. His power is hidden in the realm of which he exists, and he exists in our very nature. Sin. Man's existence in nature is that of constant rebellion against God's intention of creation. The Evil One desires destruction and death, and by all means available to him, he is relentless in his pursuit of his prey. The only sure weapon against his wiles is the written Word of God. Jesus quoted Scripture when He was tempted by the Evil One. He simply replied, "It is written, thou shalt not."

I was reading the Bible as I watched my mother, the love of my life, slowly die.

There was no sadness. Only tears of happiness. She had finally reached a place to call home forever, and there I know she is waiting and watching for her children. I preached her funeral. I would have the honor of preaching relatives' funerals or assist in them. This is a pastor's heart; knowing a life and all the things that make it what it is. We share these wonderful days as we watch each other at our best or bettering our worst. We provide for those that we love and keep our hopes and dreams alive in these short and precious days of our lives that we share for better or worse.

Chapter XI

"The Wheat and the Tares"

There were so many things I was learning it was impossible to distinguish which were good and which not so good. The county had a volunteer emergency medical service that was a basic life support service. That meant that there were no cardiac monitors on the ambulances, no drugs, just intravenous fluids for the transport of the sick and injured. The county had one ambulance, and the county board of commissioners offered little or no real help for the advancement in equipment or training. The men and women that worked would be on call, take the ambulance home with them, and respond if called. Somewhere along the way they would meet their partner and drive to the scene. It was not a perfect scenario when minutes counted, but it was the best they could do at that time. These people were true American heroes. They received a small stipend for fuel expenses but not enough to amount to anything, but that was not the reason why they did it. They were ambulance drivers like me. They would have done it for free as many did. When the EMS volunteers learned that I had a state license and had worked full time in an advanced life support service, I was immediately asked to join their efforts. I had missed this work, and it was a very needed service in this rural community.

The calls were few and infrequent, mostly transfers from the hospital to homes, but when an emergency call came, it was a real emergency. The sheriff's department dispatched the ambulance and the deputies would tell us what we needed to know en route to the scene. We did not wear uniforms, but each of us found some kind of jacket that looked similar to one another and wore it. It was not unusual to see the emergency medical technicians get out of the ambulance in their Sunday best or even in a pair of shorts and flip flops. You called, and we hauled. We were ambulance drivers, but like the rest of the country we wanted more for our community.

We wanted training and a full-time service. It was the county's destiny as I look back at it now. These men and women were solid citizens, and this was their home. It was their families that depended on this service if it was needed. So while most of us concentrated on being ambulance drivers, one or two had enough Southern political savvy to know how to get things accomplished. The same way everything was accomplished in that county: politics. Somebody had to run for county commissioner's office and elect enough men on the board to make this a priority for the county, and by golly, they did it. It took some time, but once in office they requested a one cent sales tax which funded a full-time emergency medical service and it passed. This was accomplished by these wonder men and women who gave more of themselves when nobody asked them to. But as with all good intentions, they sometimes led you in areas or endeavors you never intended to become involved in. Such was my case when they asked me to become the county's first full-time emergency medical service director. I was about to wade into the mire of the county's political abyss. The Lord sure moves in mysterious ways.

There was so much to do, and the list was abstract at times. I did not know if I needed to spit or go blind. The first thing was establishing some kind of headquarters, somewhere for the EMTs to sleep, eat, and set up some form of standard operations. I had been involved in EMS, but this was not my cup of tea. Management was a whole new deal, and I required a lot of help which I obtained from the regional state EMS office. There were requirements which pertained to housing and the storage of supplies, drugs, vehicles, as well as records of certifications and training., We needed a physician who would serve as our medical director and be responsible for approving our protocols of care and transport. This was just as big a deal for a small service as for a large one because both had to meet these requirements regardless of size. This was an awful lot of work that kept my lamp burning many late hours.

The volunteer men and women took calls until I had accomplished this initial process which allowed me to start hiring EMTs and paramedics to fill the positions. I could not have done this without their advice and their willingness to help in any way that they could. Along the way I made a few mistakes some of which I had to pay for literally.

The county Board of Commissioners let us share the volunteer fire department's building to start with and that worked well although the sleeping and living quarters lacked a good bit. However, at one of the board of commissioners' meetings an old building was mentioned as a possible source for relocation. It paid to have men on the board who were not there by accident. After several minutes of debate and voting, it was decided that we could use this building and begin operations out of that building. That was all I remember. I did not recall any instructions that said I could not move in immediately or begin building preparation. So I began to have base radio systems installed, furniture purchased, and utilities turned on in the building. I was there late one evening cleaning the carpet and doing some painting when one of the county commissioners rode by and saw the lights on in the building and stopped.

He came in looking around like he was inspecting a tenant he was about to evict. He snarled and uttered slurs under his breath. Then he began shouting at me, asking what was I doing. He was waving his arms around and pointing his finger in my face. I was doing well until he started calling me a stupid preacher. He was a deacon at the Methodist church and while I was not sure of his spiritual ethics, he was about to receive a Jesus test. I had never administered this test and this would definitely be the first time, but what the hey, that day was full of firsts. A Jesus test consisted of slapping the left side of a man's face to see if he had enough Jesus in him to present the right side of his face for testing application. It was a test that I had conceived of sometime in the past but had not yet had the reason to test it out. This was the perfect situation for testing purposes, and I was thoroughly prepared for its administration. But as all loud talking men do, he realized the seriousness of the situation. While I could not stop him from expressing his dislike in such an angry manner, I did believe I could break him of the habit. He believed he was about to receive an old fashioned Southern "butt whoopin'. He was not, but I do believe he thought that because he ran out of the building saying, "You're going to pay for this! Who do you think you are?" He was right. I would have to pay for my sins.

The county commissioner's meeting always began with the clerk calling the roll. The meeting was held in the old courthouse records office. It smelled of old books and ink. The table must have been an antique from the early 1900s, but it was beautiful and worn from the many battles that had occurred there. It was at this table that the sheriff of this county met with the police chief and made plans for using the county's jail during Martin Luther King's march in Albany. There was no doubt many such infamous hearings occurred in that room and some were legends in themselves. Millionaires and paupers alike had at one time or another made history in the decisions that were wrestled out around this table. And here I was.

Two or three of my allies on the board were absent. Maybe because it was a done deal before I arrived or they knew any bloodshed on a losing battlefield would do no one any good. These were smart men of character, and I contributed their absence to an unspoken measure of trust they placed in me to do the right thing. I would not let them down in this matter. The chairman of the board was a slow-speaking deep-voiced man who had a beautiful smile. He was a true Southern gentleman; well-educated, a successful farmer, business man, and also a deacon at his church. His introduction was interrupted by another board member who I liked a lot. He definitely was not a deacon and made no qualms about his spirituality. His profanity was often asked to be deleted from the record. He could interject profanity in a question or point in an instant and was skilled and pleased when doing so. It was said you could hear everything at these meetings except the Lord's Prayer or meat frying. I listened and expected a cussing out, but it never came. According to the record he read, where no one ever told me to move into the building, and since the radio had to be installed anyway there was no foul. But since I had taken it upon myself to move in two months sooner than they planned, I would have to pay the light bill for two months. He folded his arms and rested them on the table as if we were at the UN Cuban missile crisis session and the fate of the free world depended on my reply. He was indeed ready to wait until hell froze over for the reply. I was having a large time. I knew every eye was on me and I had the tactical advantage here. While they thought this was a showdown and a control issue, it was totally the opposite. God was in control.

I felt like laughing. I felt like crying. God's presence always catches me off guard. He shows up at the most unexpected times and takes the time to show me how silly this world is when compared to His omniscient presence. He knew the deal even before they did. There's nothing like having God on your side. It's a win-win thing. So I took full advantage of the moment. I too folded my arms and rested them on the table. I stared at the old table top and then took a pencil off the table and began writing on the yellow legal pad in front of me. I did this for at least two minutes. It must have unnerved the commissioner who had stopped by the building because he blurted out, "Well, what do you say about them beans?" I slowly raised my eyes to his and replied, "I am truly sorry I misunderstood you gentlemen's intentions and plans. That will not happen again. I think this is more than fair." And with that being said, I put my hands in my pockets and leaned back and gave them the biggest grin I could muster. The money did not matter, but since I was the director of emergency medical service department, and since I was setting everyone's salary mine just got raised a little. I sat and watched their faces. All seemed pleasantly surprised that this was over, but it was not over.

Old faithful blew his stack again, this time asking about a purchase order I had submitted for a portable suction machine.. He wanted to know why we could not use the "emesis basins" instead because we had a box full of those. He had been at the volunteer fire station taking an inventory of our supplies. I told him these were simply for patients to vomit in and that the function of the machine was to remove blood or fluids that might occlude the airway. I might as well have spit in his face. He went off. He said nothing else was going to be bought until they had somebody that knew what in the hell he was talking about. I didn't say anything. Why? Why argue with a man that I knew was against everything that I was trying to do. I handed the purchase request to the clerk and asked her to please order the piece of equipment, and I left. I heard him ranting as I walked down the hallways of the court house. That was the last I heard from this county commissioner since his initial visit to the EMS building, but a paramedic crew I had hired told me something about him that changed the way he treated the county's new EMS service forever.

This crew had responded to an automobile accident where he had been driving his truck on a dirt and after rounding a curve ran into the back of a logging truck that had stalled out. One of the small pine trees had crashed through the windshield and broken his jaw and caused massive facial trauma. One of the paramedics had borrowed a portable suction machine from his full-time EMS employer that we could use until we got one. It was a state-required piece of equipment.

The seasoned paramedic used it to keep this man's throat clear of teeth, blood, glass, and pine bark. God had shut this man's mouth. In a couple of weeks I received an interoffice message from the board that I no longer had to wait for the county board of commissioners' approval to purchase any item less than one thousand dollars. The action was passed unanimously by the county commissioners.

Now I have no idea why God allowed this to happen to this man. I mean accidents are just that, accidents. God does not kill anyone by accident. Everything I've ever read about His judgment against man is pretty clear. God's intentions are obvious. The parting of the Red Sea, the fire and brimstone falling from the sky, the angel with a sword, all of these events God makes personal, but not accidental. Man will never stumble into the judgment of God but He does allow man to learn from his mistakes and change his way of thinking. So it was with this man. He became the department's most faithful supporter.

The news at the time kept showing Jimmy Swaggart's tearful face all day long. The pitiful accounts of PTL's Jim and Tammy Faye Baker and Swaggart's transgressions were rolled together like the previews of a new movie. Everybody was talking. This coupled with the pedophile charges against some Catholic priest and it was as if the men in the ministry had taken a direct hit. It was sad to me. I had knelt in front my television and repented many times following Jimmy's preaching. He was and is in my view the best evangelist that I've ever heard. No one can deny his accomplishments for the Lord in his evangelistic efforts. He has mastered the ability to preach, and his ministry was a machine that was cranking out every possible avenue of sharing the gospel. It might have well been the biggest evangelistic effort by any one individual ever. His crusades were recorded and shown all over the world and still are today. Yet in the crescendo of his ministry he was finding himself publically apologizing for moral failure. It was on the lips of the world one Sunday afternoon and even found its way to our little country church.

We were having a lunch that afternoon at the church. I can't recall the event, but I do remember that it was a beautiful day and there was good attendance. I had been busy doing something in the church and was at the end of the lunch line. I had fixed my plate and was walking outside to sit at one of the tables. I walked around a huge oak tree toward the tables. On the other side of the tree, sitting at a table, were Aunt Kelly, Aunt Betsy, and Aunt Ida May. Now none of these women were my aunts, but everybody in the church called the elderly widows "aunt." I don't know why and thought it was strange at first but found myself complying in this colloquial custom. It didn't hurt anything and these women were in their seventies. It was a way of paying a measure of respect to them I suppose. But I never expected to hear the conversation these matriarchs of the faith were having that afternoon.

Aunt Betsy, holding her fork loaded with greens and corn bread in one hand stopped in mid-effort and said, "Listen to me, I've always heard a hard pecker ain't got no conscious, I reckon it's true." The other women howled with laughter saying, "Oh Betsy, you stop it now." I almost choked on my sweet 'tater pie. I could not believe what I had heard. That would have never been something I would have expected one of these ladies to say, but they did and I was finding it unbelievable. I had heard these women give beautiful Christian testimonies and sing the hymns with such devotion and sincerity, so to hear their base conversation was startling. I thought at least they could have chosen a more acceptable word for the description of the male anatomy. I could not believe it. I would have expected them to be talking about how it must have broken the heart of Swaggart's wife and how was she ever going to forgive him. This was what I expected from elderly ladies of the faith; a conversation about restoration and forgiveness.

This is the biblical principle on which the gospel exists. Forgiveness is joined with forgetting at the spiritual hip. One cannot exist without the other. While the church has the responsibility to govern the behavior of its members and officers, this is to be done in the spirit of restoration not destruction. That is the message of Christ, restoring a fallen nature to original creation by the shed blood of its Savior upon the cross of Calvary. It is my only hope and my greatest belief. Yet the human tendency is to require the one caught in a fault some great measure of public suffering and shameful humiliation. The self- righteous who are quick to condemn and slow to forget are usually the ones who misunderstand the ministry of the church. Oh, they may be on every board in the church and put the most in the offering plates, but they shed no tears for the spiritually wounded or the one overtaken by the Wicked One. Make no mistake about it; the reason why all of us find ourselves in places of shortcomings is because while we may sporadically stroll on the spiritual mountain top, Satan is constantly about his business of robbing, killing, and destroying any spiritual growth that we may have obtained by the grace of God.

I walked toward the table acting as if I never heard their conversation and thought about the spiritual reality of what had just happened. I had learned an invaluable lesson about the nature of mankind. On this side of the grave there is no place where we can escape the human nature of man. It is what it is and change can only be brought about by the renewing of our mind through God's Word. I realized that every moment of every day there is an unseen evil that resides in our spiritual DNA, and it is the sin nature. We are born in it, live with it, and wrestle with it until we die. Men and women alike will always come short of the glory of God by their own efforts. It is only by divine intervention that we can overcome the vast avenues of darkness we all are lured to travel. That reality is seen in religious history from King David to Jimmy Swaggart to the latest scandal. It is seen in the secular world from Roosevelt to Clinton, from the poorest to the richest. There are no exceptions. The wages of sin is death, and I was about to get in the death business as a deputy coroner.

The coroner needed a deputy to assist him when he was unavailable to respond to the scene of a death. That was all I needed, one more job to learn. The educational requirement for a coroner in the state of Georgia was simply being elected. You were required to attend a three-day school at the state's training facility to learn the paperwork, the resources, and the policies available, but it was a most modest requirement. The medical examiner for the state crime lab would require certain procedures and protocols to be followed and the Georgia Bureau of Investigation was contacted when certain scenarios of death occurred. In the state of Georgia the coroner is really just the legal guardian of the deceased person ,making sure that the deceased's property and cause of death are handled properly. It was an easy and interesting job, but I was finding the on-call time very limiting on my free time. I had so little as it was, and this addition was not helping things. My fellow ministers, upon learning of my roles as EMS director and deputy coroner, said of me, "I hatched 'em, patched 'em, and dispatched 'em." I guess in a way they were right, but during the rush I got lost in all the business and the years quickly passed by. Along the way, life came and left, but as long as I could take the time to live a little I did well.

Chapter XII

"The Water into Wine"

"We have gathered here today to join this woman and this man in holy matrimony. If any man knows of any just reason why these two may not be joined as husband and wife, let him speak now or forever hold his peace."

I don't know how many weddings I've done over the years. It is not something that I find important to count, but it would be interesting to see how many lasted in the bliss of matrimony. I have had some experiences in this line of the ministry that must not be unique to only me. Certainly other ministers could recount such stories of the weddings they did, and the ones they did not do. I guess I was different than most Baptist preachers. I would marry a man and woman that had been married before. It would have been more than hypocritical for me to adopt a sudden change of spiritual conviction when my own life was totally the opposite. In doing this, I raised a few eyebrows across the ministerial community and even within the congregation. However, it was always amazing to me when this situation affected one's own children how quickly it suddenly didn't seem so awful. Circumstances were different in one particular case, and there was really nothing that could be done to save the first marriage. It was not thier child's fault.

Ministers now will not marry someone that is not a member of their church. They state that the couple can go to the courthouse and a justice of the peace can perform the marriage thereby relinquishing them from owning any part of its success or failure or spiritual correctness. I'm not sure and have no statistical data to support what I'm about to say, but maybe this is a contributing factor for most couples living together. They see marriage as unnecessary. If the church has closed the door of human contact with the outside world, allowing only its own kind the privilege of a God-acknowledged effort to begin a new life together, what are they to do?

I know what Jesus said about marriage. I know what Paul wrote about a man being the husband of one woman. I know these things. I just believe that God's intent was to show that the only way a divorce was acceptable was if the other person was guilty of detrimental intent of harm or betrayal. I do believe it was, is, and will forever be the will of God that a man and a woman joined in marriage should exert every strength and reason to remain married for the entirety of their lives. That was the deal with Adam and Eve, but sin was allowed to destroy God's perfect creation.

Through the physical and mental intent of Eve and Adam's actions, they destroyed the perfect union between God and man. Sin entered the world and death with it. Had it ended there, and thank God it did not, that would have been all she wrote. But Christ died for the sins of humanity and that perfect union was restored. The Creator and the creation were again united under the crimson flow of Calvary's cross. When Christ hung upon the cross He not only said, "I will do this," He did it! He followed God's plan of restoration and paid an immeasurable sin debt for all the Adams and Eves of the world. Satan's effort to destroy the union was finally defeated, and Jesus referred to the church as His bride. How hard is that to understand?

For the love of God, Jesus Christ of Nazareth did for marriage what no other religious foundation of the world could do. He gave them a chance to find the person He intended for them to be with in the first place. There seems to be a great debate about same-sex marriage today. The creation of marriage was for the procreation of the human species and the development of the family. While it seems flippant to say this, had God intended man to marry man He would have placed Adam and Steve in the garden and not Adam and Eve. The union of same-sex marriages accommodates social and economic fairness of today's society, but it fails to meet what the Christian believes the initial intent of marriage to be.

I do not understand homosexuality. I, like everyone, know gay men and women who live their lives around us. Some are members of our family. We love them. The famous saying, "Love the sinner but hate the sin" is to me a slight to God. For if gay men and women can read the Word of God and still maintain their lifestyle and their beliefs well, that's between them and God isn't it? What does it matter what I think about their sexual orientation? What does it matter what I think about their soul and their well-being? If they constantly feel that I judge them as deviants or lesser human beings, how could I ever receive fair judgment from them about who and what I am and what I believe? We spend far too much time attempting to be God and far too little time trying to be Christ like. Every soul will end up in the hands of a loving and righteous God, and He will do what's right without exception.

Doing what is right is not as easy as it sounds, especially when you don't know what to do. There have been couples that have come to me asking me to marry them when they were already secretly married. Their parents and family did not know they were married, and now they had somehow found it time or it was acceptable to make it public. I simply asked them to tell their parents they were married, and then I would perform the ceremony. My reasoning behind such a request was that it gave them the chance to do what was right by their parents. Uncles, aunts, and busybody in-laws, who would use this information as a topic to discuss one's character and spiritual well-being, would be left out of the equation. Private issues of why they had done this were not for public consumption. Consumption would play a part of the first wedding I ever did, however.

I met the bride to be at her house and she introduced her brother to me. He was at that time the youngest mayor in the state of Georgia.It was also rumored that he was the youngest cocaine addict in the county. He had been helping on the county's volunteer ambulance service prior to my arrival in the county, but recent encounters with the gentlemen of the Georgia highway patrol had altered his driving privileges. The bride had informed me that there would be champagne at the wedding reception and asked if it would be a problem. I told her I would try not to drink too much, and we laughed about it, but I knew there would be questions from some of the church folk. They say the only difference between Methodist and Baptist church folk is that the Methodist will at least speak to one another in the liquor store. The Baptists, however, believe that the consumption of any fermented wine or alcoholic beverage is a sign of possession cured only by a second dunkin' and possible exorcism. I sensed that this might apply to any minister that conducted a wedding where these evil spirits may be served as well. I was not wrong.

The news that I had accepted the privilege of performing the marriage ceremony had traveled faster than expected. I stopped at a gas station to get some fuel and the black man who pumped gas and changed tires there knew I was going to officiate the wedding. I had not even gotten home. How in the world?

The silence of that Southern spring night was interrupted several times by blaring telephone rings; church members fishing for the positive, absolute confirmation that I indeed was going to do this. They were so sweet. They did everything but plainly ask me if I was going to do the wedding. They walked all the way around the tree and shook every limb on it but never plainly asked. They were minding their own business. Ring. Ring. Ring. *Do not ask for whom the bell tolls preacher boy. It tolls for thee,* I said to myself knowing that this person on the other end of the line had enough gall to ask me, "Boxers or briefs?" I studied his verbal ploy, and he was a master at the art of conversation. He would be laughing and talking about something so far removed and then gradually ease up to the wedding matter like an old hound wanting to be petted. You can learn a lot about people by paying attention to the way they talk, but you can learn more about them from the way they listen. He was a man that heard what he wanted to hear, and I knew that, so I prayed for strength to bridle my tongue.

"Did ya hear so and so is getting married, preacher?" he asked. "Hold on a minute," I told him. "I'll be right back. I need to tend to the children." I did this several times. Every time he was about to ask me if I was going to do the wedding, I would ask for a recess from the conversation. I increased his wait time by two minute increments on each occasion. He waited on that phone like a hawk waiting on a tree limb for an opportunity to seize his prey, me. On that last wait cycle I was beating on an empty pot in the kitchen and told him I was getting ready to fix up a pot of stew. I was too. I was hungry. Then I returned to the phone and complied with his determined effort and gave him the answer an unknown multitude was waiting on. Yes, I was indeed going to do the wedding. He hung up so fast it was borderline rude. I laughed and laughed and then I dialed some of the church members phones I thought he might be broadcasting to, and sure enough telephone lines were busy. I had increased Ma Bell's profits that night somewhat.

There was an additional aspect to this matter that I had not reckoned on in making the decision to do this thing. This particular family was very well off and belonged to its own political faction. The grandfather had been prominent in the judicial system and had a colorful history in his own right. His name was familiar in the law offices of Georgia. He had been investigated for being an accomplice to murder on one occasion, but the charge was dismissed because three witnesses of the crime suddenly disappeared and were never seen again. He was the wealthiest man in the county during his lifetime. There were a great many stories. There were so many stories there was no way they could all be true. Yet there was enough truth in them, that years after his death, the mention of his name still caused people to hesitate before they spoke against this family. I did not know all of this history about this man and his family when I met with this young couple. I was told story after story during the weeks leading up to the time of the wedding. It was as if the people of the county resented the young pastor for being associated with the likes of these people. It was for many unacceptable, but for many others they saw it as a ministry of the church. I know that was how I saw it.

The wedding was as fancy as they come. Horse-drawn carriages and servants dressed in the colonial manner served the guests cool drinks and pâté. Music was played by a live string quartet, and ducks swam across a nearby pond. Seven or eight young beagle pups had the run of the place, and the children were laughing and running after the pups. It was like a scene out of a movie slowly playing out that beautiful afternoon. I expected Rhett Butler and Miss Scarlett to sashay across the green grass. It was the most beautiful wedding I ever officiated, but it got ugly, real ugly, real fast.

The rehearsal had been an event in itself. There was the pre-rehearsal brunch and casting where everyone would stand, turn at a certain time, and do certain things when certain music was played. Nothing was left to chance. The wedding director could have been a Hollywood director as she shouted commands and prompts to the various characters in the wedding party. The choreographed movements were not left to chance. Stage markers of different colors marked where certain people were to be at certain times of the wedding. Every detail was approved or declined based upon the director's artistic intent at the moment. This person had come all the way from Miami for this so there would be strict compliance. No one questioned her authority or knowledge as to what was acceptable according to the latest fashion in weddings. She kept saying this wedding would make social history in the state. She was not wrong. This wedding would go down in the archives of "I dos, I don'ts, and I believe I wouldn't do that if I were you."

The bride was absolutely beautiful. She was a pretty girl anyway, but for some reason women on their wedding day have a special glow about them. I have seen many brides, but I never saw one, no matter how simple the ceremony or attire, that was not absolutely gorgeous. This young lady could have been a model for any wedding magazine. The weather cooperated beautifully. It was all recorded for historical reference as three cameras were placed at strategically chosen places. The sound engineers had placed microphones on the performers. The wedding party wore wireless microphones hidden from the view of the photographers' lenses. There were two photographers who spoke to each other in some sort of coded hand messages. I tried to decode this method of communication, but I saw no rhyme or reason in their frantic gestures. They were Chinese, and spoke in their native language as they followed the wedding program and documented their planned shots on a portable easel board. Everything was cued up and ready and we all awaited the release of four dozen white doves which signaled to everyone the start of the wedding that would go down in the social history of the great state of Georgia.

The wedding guests were seated. The doves were released and the sound of their flapping wings filled the moment of silence during the musical prelude that was playing. It was timed perfectly, and the audience gasped at the beauty of these doves flying over their heads into the crystal blue sky. Well, forty-seven doves flew. The one that chose to take a stroll in the green grass found seven beagles in hot pursuit. This ended with the biggest puppy carrying the bloody dove in his mouth like a prize trying to hide under one of the chairs of a wedding guest. This caused each guest in the area to jump up, trying to keep the blood and wet feathers off their clothes. They looked like popcorn popping up. This was handled quickly as the director had assigned rescue managers to deal with the dogs and birds. The guilty killer was apprehended and taken away wrapped in a large towel. The other puppies scattered into the nearby sapling pines barking as they ran. What could have been a disaster was handled perfectly. There is nothing like preparation to guarantee a proper exchange of wedding vows. However, there is no preparation for the unexpected behavior of human beings.

The youngest mayor must have felt slighted in all this wedding hullaballoo. He was assigned no major role in his sister's wedding. His only task was to walk down the stone pathway beside one of the bridesmaids. Just walk. At no time was he to speak or make any physical contribution to the wedding march which he did in notable fashion. As they came down the aisle he stood in front of the whole assembly and shouted, referring to groom, "The ole boy gonna get a good piece tonight," and slapped the matron of honor on her bottom. Imagine seeing a hundred or so sets of human eyeballs suddenly expand to their maximum potential. It looked like a Walt Disney cartoon. I had to bite my lip to keep from laughing at the sight of those guests' abhorrent reaction to this vulgarity. The gasps were audible in the next county.

Then suddenly the cousin of the bride turned and hit the young mayor in the gut so hard it caused the him to instantaneously empty his bladder right there on the stone walkway in front of God and everybody. I know the average amount of urine the human body can hold, but I had no idea that it could ever hold such a vast volume as that which spilled and puddled on the walkway. I could actually see the entire reflection of that big sun which brought the light of day to this wedding. A small scuffle broke out around the young mayor and the wedding party. Men were slipping and sliding in the urine as they jostled for the upper hand in this matter. Their fancy foot work was splashing urine onto the ankles and shoes of those nearby and the cries for mercy went up as if these people were standing on the deck of the Titanic.

Through this turmoil I caught a glimpse of the young bride's trembling hands standing at the back of the crowd. The arrangement of flowers she held violently shook as she was holding back the tears. How she did this I'll never know, but she stood there in character and position waiting for the wedding to continue as if this was a planned part of the service.

The Chinese photographers were signaling each other so rapidly they looked like they were kneading dough for a batch of pastries. When one raised his camera to take a picture, the mother of the groom slapped his face and screamed, "What are you doing? Have you lost your jay-pan mind?" He finally made a hand signal I could understand as well as everybody else there. A big red-headed boy grabbed the photographer around the neck and began to pound the top of his head. This brought the other photographer in full gallop to rescue his partner from this ole boy's headlock. Then suddenly there were so many defensive and offensive moves being made it was hard to tell who was hitting who and for what. The battle of Gettysburg saw no greater deeds of its son's valor defending the honor of the South than did this skirmish started by Georgia's youngest drunken politician.

I've married people on mountain tops, in churches, in hotels, and in action buildings. Why I even performed a wedding ceremony for a physician and his bride in the middle of a shift in an emergency room. I have officiated at weddings of splendor, and I've done weddings where beanie-weenies were served. I've had grooms wear cowboy hats and NASCAR jackets. I've heard the song "Angel Kisses" played so many times I've prayed for a power failure on more than one occasion.

Some couples remain married and some do not, but it is never the ceremony which determines their marital bliss. Those who stay together are people who find that person God intended them to live with forever, and they protect that relationship with God's help at all costs. It is only when one realizes that the other spouse will continue unrestrained in their physical and mental intent to harm the relationship that destroys homes and families. It is also the intent of the heart which will spur the man or woman to be what the other desires. A mutual desire to see their lives offering to each other the best each person has to give. Many say "I do" and never do. Many say "I will" but they won't. The failure to do all that is necessary to protect the relationship must be realized before it's too late in a relationship. This failure will have long-lasting effects on many lives for many years to come. I know.

The duties of EMS director, deputy coroner, and pastor of this church kept me busy for a few years, and then it was time to go. I loved this church and the beautiful Southern norms that dotted everyday life. I loved the ministry there, and I can still recall the faces and names of most of the people. They left on my heart and mind valuable riches as they tutored me in the business of a preacher boy becoming a man of God. I never liked to use the title reverend in front of my name. There has never been anything reverent about my life.

Chapter XIII

"Revelations"

I t is easy to look back on the past and realize there are things you would have done differently. Different choices you would have made, different directions you would have chosen. But while it was not perfect, it offered grand experiences. Experience comes in subtle ebbs and flows of life. Each measured by the degree of error one perceives in the right and wrong of things. Yet it is more often the wrong that brings about the next right than the degree of accomplishment. As I look back on the churches that I pastored, I realize the common denominator was the need. People need a pastor. It is the most important job a man could do in this life. The greatest need in our world today is the need for men of God, men that He has selected regardless of preparation or prestige, regardless of degree or pedigree. The fabric that will be used to fashion the society of our great-grandchildren is the adorned men of God selected by His call and summoned by His Spirit. But where are they now? Where are the evangelists that will deliver the message, "This sayeth the Lord" and allow God the liberty of their lives to use them as He sees fit? Today there are annual press releases of pastors of great churches who have been caught up in some vile sin. The church is reduced to evangelists running reruns of revival meetings they had many years ago. Today the church is more interested in getting bigger instead of getting better, believing that getting bigger is the will of

God. I would rather be in a church getting better at living the kind of life that is pleasing to God than the mega-churches of mediocrity; for the dangers facing the church now are far greater than they ever have been.

There is a man named Steven Greer who is teaching seminars that instruct his students on how to contact aliens on UFOs. Steven Greer is an emergency room physician that no longer practices medicine but leads a group of former military pilots and officers who have publically stated they have seen UFOs or aliens. The name of his group's effort is called "The Disclosure Project," and they are requesting that the United States release all of the information it has about UFOs and extraterrestrials. There are many videos describing this effort on YouTube entitled "The Day Before Disclosure" or "The Disclosure Project," some which will lead you to Dr. Steven Greer's efforts. He insists that these crafts appear during these CSETI sessions. While his viewing numbers are modest, he claims he has met with CIA members and presidents and briefed them on his group's progress. He also states that his goal is to meet with world leaders and act as an ambassador for these alien beings. One might dismiss his efforts as insignificant, but one should remember the railings Hitler started in pubs where he would shout as he presented his outline for *Mein Kampf*. The deception Hitler cast over the minds of the German people cost the world dearly.

It took millions of lives, billions of dollars, and human sufferings beyond description to destroy his influence. It spread like wildfire reaching every continent and scarring every person. The scars are still there, and thank God for that, because they are reminders of the sleeping conscience of humanity. A humanity that chose to ignore Hitler's meager beginnings until nations began to fall.

The warfare for the minds of mankind has already began as the spiritual conscience of the church slumbers in selective silence, choosing to ignore these meager beginnings of the antichrist movement. These beings and craft have been sighted by professional pilots, astronauts, children, police officers, and just about every government of the world. The Mexican Air Force showed the world a fleet of these craft moving at unbelievable speeds and direction. These are not practice runs for the invasion of the world but rather the saber rattling of the Evil One. The battle is not for the resources of the earth or for the abductions of human beings. The battle is for the conscious mind of humanity. Each occurrence is perfectly executed in a manner and deed so as to present to man scientific possibilities and not spiritual realities.

It is in the arena of science in which the Evil One will dazzle the minds of mankind. Current known projects demonstrate this has already begun as the Hedron Collider in Sweden seeks to capture the God Particle in its efforts to reproduce the moment of creation. The creation of black holes and a host of unknown sciences lie hidden in the bed of secret experimentation. While we consider the absurdity of these things being true or non-existent, let us remember President Truman had to be informed there was a weapon that had just been invented which could end the war quickly. This was, of course, the result of the Manhattan Project, the atomic bomb. President Truman wrote a handwritten note authorizing its release, but he noted, "Not to be dropped until after August 2nd." Timing was everything. The vice president of the United States did not know of the atomic weapon's existence until it became necessary for him to know two weeks following Roosevelt's death. Timing was everything.

Therefore let us look at the current acknowledgement that the church has made concerning these UFO events. The Vatican released an official statement saying that alien life was indeed possible. While it offered no exact explanation for the story of creation, the fall of man, and the apocalyptic influence of such a statement, it made the statement. However, the Catholic religion cannot speak for the body of believers who do not embrace Catholicism. The various religions of the world and its beliefs are so abstract to each other it is hard to see a common avenue of reason except in science. For it was in science that the progress of man was experienced in every culture. It was in science that religions and nations seek influence, power, and understanding. It will be to this hunger for knowledge that the Antichrist will feed overwhelming evidence questioning the very existence of God and the only begotten Son Christ Jesus. Raised by atheist parents, Dr. Steven Greer tells his students that the first thing they must lay down is their spiritual acknowledgement of Christ as a savior and the trinity of the Godhead; God the Father, God the Son, and God the Holy Ghost.

He uses scientific terminology foreign to known physics to describe the manifestation of these alien creatures and their ability to travel millions of light years, warping time and dimension. He produces photographs and recordings on various scientific monitors but insists personal experience is the best proof the students will acquire. While he presents this technology as cutting edge and necessary to communicate with the aliens, he fails to realize that these creatures have been communicating with the minds of man for many years as demons and fallen angels. He attempts to describe the boundary between the physical and spiritual world and how it is crossed, yet he fails to honor the reason for its existence and the consequences of violating the great divide.

He states that the military tries to intervene and interrupt the sessions of contact using their own electromagnetic devises as jets and helicopters vector into the air space. He also claims that a group called the Magnificent Seven have kept secret the true details of Roswell New Mexico where a UFO crashed in 1948. He and others describe a vast network of wealthy and powerful people whose goal is to squash every UFO incident and withhold acknowledgment of their existence from the world and its leaders. Again, timing is everything.

This brings the central question to the forefront, why? Why would alien creatures travel such distances simply to dart in and out of our world, toy with our nuclear abilities, and yet reveal themselves to common people? Why would such creatures honor an agreement of universal segregation? What would be the restraining force so powerful as to prevent undeniable acknowledgment of contact between man and alien life? The answers to these questions and many more is the fact that God has deemed it not yet time for their unveiling.

The events in the book of Revelation are symbolic gestures of what theologians say are events which will occur in this world in the latter days. They use the books of Daniel, Ezekiel, and others to portray their understanding of Scripture concerning these events. While I am no student of eschatology, I am reminded that the descendants of the people who wrote the Old Testament crucified Christ believing they were doing God a service. In fact they really were, they just didn't know it. So with a measure of ignorance men then and now have moved toward God's plan since creation. It is on God's time, and God's time is always on time.

Therefore, the most important knowledge of what will happen at a certain time is what happens in our daily lives. That is the time which we are accountable for and in which we can remedy our deeds and conduct. The only way to die right is to live right because there is not a lot of time in between the two. I have watched many souls leave this world and many stay which defied physical injury or illness. The central factor in both cases has always been that it was in the hands of a benevolent, loving God. In His hands all were cradled and protected until the appointed time for their souls to cross from the physical world to the spiritual realm. As I cared for their bodies and pastored their souls, I did the best I could do. There will come a time when I will give an account for all I did and did not do, all that I was, and all that I was not. In all these things I was honored with a brief glimpse of the beauty of God's creation, man.

As sojourners making our way to the spiritual reunion with God, we pass many who are wounded in their efforts from the journey. Broken hearts, broken minds, and scattered pieces of their lives lie along the highways of our path. Many times their physical and spiritual well-being will be determined by our actions and our deeds of assistance. The rules of the road are simple. We are not responsible for the many crashes, only the one God places in our path. We are protected by God's powerful law of grace. In human law, the Good Samaritan Law, states that if someone (a non-professional) causes harm while attempting to render aide to a fallen victim, the person is not libel for his or her actions. We are not the Great Physician. Some have convinced mankind we can be Christ like. We cannot. It is a spiritual paradox. We are sinful creatures. Jesus was sinless.

Jesus was and still is God's Christ. He was visible proof of God's existence and in His entire human life He was not less than God. He was the only begotten of the heavenly Father, and this was recognized by those who met Him. He did incredible miracles and revealed to humanity the vast dimensions of God's love for us. His true identity was recognized by every dark being He encountered. They recognized Him and plead for mercy as He drove them from the presence of tortured human beings. The church was first called "The Way." Many are lost in this journey of life and simply need someone to point the way.

The direction for the course of humanity was plotted even before the world was created. The science of carbon dating measures materials in earthly time, and science uses advanced computer UV-light waves to estimate the galaxies and universes millions of light years away in celestial time Yet in the fathoms of eternity these are mere glimpses of what was and what will be. The black holes, which scientists struggle to define and understand, were described in Scripture in the Old testament. These are the prisons for some of the fallen angels of God. The crashing and exploding universes were nothing more than the reflection of a battlefield where God's battling angels drove from God's presence the defiant followers of Satan.

The places and nature of their imprisoned existence varies according to the purpose of God's plan for humanity. For in humanity God would find within its generations a group of souls whom He would use to reveal His true nature and purpose—God's desire for a being with rational thought who chose to love Him for His marvelous creations spanning eternity. A humanity that would exist in its natural span of time, and within that measure of time, have the free will to choose to believe or not. There would be no forced acceptance of spiritual matters, but man would be given every needed tool to explore and confirm God's existence and His holy character. Man was created in the image of God. It is in the image of God, not a replication of God. In that part of the eternal soul God allowed man to plot his own course, his own destination in eternity. So how long shall this soul search for God continue ?

The popular topic with every modern-day evangelist who wants to be a prophet of today is, "Are these the last days?" or "Is this the end of time?" They drag the poor carcass of Israel around like a doormat and lay it at the apocalyptic vestibule of judgment. I have never seen such dramatic efforts to attract attention to themselves. They hurl Scripture and woes on the covers of books and church signs, depicting themselves as most knowledgeable on these matters. Yet on the most pressing issue of spiritual significance they remain conspicuously silent. In this most challenging time for the spiritual children of God, and possibly the greatest time of deception, the church remains cautiously quiet when addressing the issue of alien existence and to a certain extent rightly so. The main purpose of the church is to spread the message of Christ and His redemptive atonement for the sins of mankind.

The church and its pastors are there for the edification of the saints, teaching the body of believers the fundamentals of the faith, and living a life before them as examples of followers of Christ. Yet its responsibility also rests in making them aware and prepared for the most unbelievable attack Satan has ever launched against the church.

It will be Satan's most masterful design that will reveal only glimpses of its true author. He will in some manner of disclosure reveal to the world these aliens as beings from far away star systems or even from other dimensions of time. They will provide to humans undeniable evidence of their existence, but they will deny the redemption in Christ. The time of this event is in the hands of God the Father. Jesus said He did not know the Father's decision on this matter. What is the church to do concerning this possible deluge of deception which will challenge the faith of even the elect ?

The answer is, of course, to keep on doing what it is doing. Satan began his beguiling effort with Eve in the garden. His desire to destroy the mind of man continues even after the soul has recognized Christ as Savior. Thoughts so vile and far removed from a Christian's behavior suddenly leap in our thoughts for unexplained reasons. This is the nature of sin that abides in these mortal bodies, born there after the fall of man. The church addresses this as instructed in Scripture. It has been doing a very effective job of presenting God's word of instruction. The pastor follows the Holy Spirit's leadership in shepherding the flock by preaching forgiveness and restoration. The danger of this final great deception by Satan is that it will overpower many shallow planted seeds, meaning that millions and millions of souls that were presented the gospel, heard its message, and were close to accepting it will instead believe what physically stands before their eyes. The portion of faith required to believe God's Word for many will diminish to such low levels that it could be compared to believing in Satan Claus or a fairy tale. Praying and petitioning God in Jesus name will cease for these uprooted souls, and they will perish by the millions in their sins. The church must keep doing what it is doing and asking for His power to do it.

There are very few souls in the history of mankind that has caught a glimpse of God's power. There has only been one instance during my Christian life when I physically felt God's power. That's not to say I have not on many occasions felt the leadership and comfort of the Holy Spirit's presence. Rather this was a physical confirmation that He, God Himself, confirmed beyond a doubt that

He was aware of me and I of Him. It lasted all of three seconds, if that long, but it has been an anchor and was for me the sole proof of His existence.

I had been asked to preach at a revival service a local church was having. Ministers from surrounding churches spoke on different nights of the week. I vividly remember the message I preached. It was about the night we ran from our childhood home, fleeing the drunken destruction of its demise, my father. I recalled his life as a boy soldier and the horror of war that he must have endured. I told the story of the night we ran from my father's insanity. I recall it was a moving service, but there was no unusual spiritual phenomenon. It was a message about love and forgiveness. It was a message of hope and promise.

The invitation was given and no one came forward as I recall, but I am not sure about that. Another pastor stood at the altar for counseling and prayer, but I do not remember any affirmations of faith or testimony. As the service concluded, I walked toward the back door. down the center aisle of the sanctuary. All of a sudden a simple looking man stood in front of me. He had on khaki trousers and a green plaid shirt. He was non-descriptive in that he looked like any other man that had worked that day, cleaned up, and came to church. He was by himself. I remember every word he said to me. He said, "Preacher, I've been waiting all my life to hear what you preached tonight. May God bless you." With that he extended his hand, and we shook hands. The moment we grasped hands I could see in his eyes he was feeling what I was feeling. Both of us were speechless. There was no shouting, no acknowledgement from either of us about what we were experiencing. It was as if we both looked into each other's eyes and saw the affirmation that something incredible was happening. When our hands grasped, there was a surge of power that went from my hand to the top of my head and down to the soles of my feet. It felt like an electrical shock except it vibrated every bone in my body. I had worked as an electrician's helper and had been shocked by 240 watts before, but this was different. It was spiritual not physical. It went to the depths of my soul, and that sensation remains as vivid in my memory today as it did those many years ago. I believe it was the Heavenly Father confirming a ministry of forgiveness and love for me.

The man released my hand and asked me, "Did you feel that?" "Yes, I did." I replied. He turned and was gone. I never knew his name and never saw him again. No one there could tell me his name as they had not paid attention to who I was speaking with. One day in heaven I will ask his name, but I think I already know it.

The church must continue in its labor for the harvesting of souls. The Lord said the harvest is plentiful but the laborers are few. The church must select its pastors as the Holy Spirit directs and then provide a spiritual body of believers to assist and support their efforts for the Lord. Both church and pastor will give an account of this precious time we have left. The end times may be many, many generations down the road but not for everyone. Many will spend their last day on this earth never knowing it was their last day. I have removed the shoes of people who had placed them on their feet that morning expecting to remove them that night. They never did. John, who wrote the book of Revelation and saw all the horrors of the tribulation to come, said in the very last sentence of the Bible, "… even so come Lord Jesus."

Since the night I ran down that dark road with my family, I've been mindful of the uncertainties which lay ahead. That night as we ran for safety, I ran with those that I loved. I ran with my family. One day when God sends His Son Christ Jesus to come and get His church, His family, we shall run together. We shall not run as vagabonds, refugees, or in fear for we have a home He has prepared for us. The journey will be over and our lives affecting others judged, good or bad, intentional or unintentional, and that is the truth, so help us God.

Just as the history of man has undisclosed details which influenced the course of humanity, so are the details which influenced each of us to do what we did. The push and pulls of life come from every direction. Expectations of parents motivate their children while false promises destroy the dreams and hopes of a people. Therefore the intention must be weighed by the measure of truth within any influence. It is easy to ask "What were you thinking?", but it requires a divine reckoning to know, only God knows why a man chooses to do the things he does. Searching through the pockets of the dead offers no voice of reason, nor plea of defense, there is only silence.

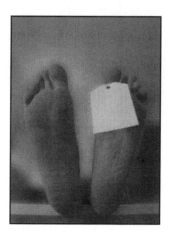